Missions

The Biblical Motive and Aim

by John M. L. Young

Crown & Covenant
PUBLICATIONS

© 1962 John M. L. Young
© 2007 Crown & Covenant Publications
7408 Penn Ave., Pittsburgh, PA 15208
info@crownandcovenant.com
www.crownandcovenant.com

The publishers gratefully acknowledge the generosity of Jane Young in this
publication of her husband's work.

ISBN: 978-1-884527-22-7

Library of Congress Control Number: 2007924835

Printed in the United States of America
at McNaughton & Gunn, Inc., Michigan

Originally published as a series of pamphlets entitled *The Motive and Aim of Missions*
by World Presbyterian Missions, Wilmington, Del., 1964.

Table of Contents

Preface

One of the best known China missionaries was Canadian Presbyterian Jonathan Goforth. He began his missionary labors in the late 1880s. During his visit in Manchuria, the famous revival occurred. He remained active well into the 1930s. While visiting in Japan with another Canadian missionary family, he had frequent talks with their high-school-age son. That son of missionary parents felt at that time that the Lord would have him return to the Far East with His gospel.

That high schooler was John M. L. Young. Dr. Young is now with the Lord after a lifetime full of service to Him. I owe a great debt of gratitude to John M. L. Young on at least three counts that I will enumerate below. Let me say here, however, that merely encouraging the publication of this book and writing this new introduction could never repay that enormous debt, as you will see.

Background

John M. L. Young was born in Hamheung, Korea, of Canadian Presbyterian missionary parents. He received his grade school education there. Later, the family lived in Kobe, Japan. In Kobe, he graduated from the Canadian Academy. He received the degrees of B. A. and M. A. from Acadia University in Wolfille, Nova Scotia. He attended Westminster Theological Seminary in Philadelphia for two years and graduated in 1938 from Faith Theological Seminary, then located in Wilmington, Delaware. He was ordained to the ministry in the Bible Presbyterian Church. Later, after a merger of denominations, he was a minister of the Reformed Presbyterian Church Evangelical Synod, and, after that body joined the Presbyterian Church in America, he served as a ministerial member there as well.

Missionary Service

Dr. Young and his wife, Jean Elder, served as missionaries in Harbin, Manchuria, from 1938 to 1941; he then served as an organizing pastor of a church in the United States from 1942 to 1948. In 1948, the Youngs went to Nanking, China, but had to leave at the end of that year due to the communist takeover. They moved to Japan, and, in 1949, Dr. Young became co-founder of the Japan Christian Theological Seminary, where he taught systematic theology and was president until 1966. In those 18 years, he helped plant three churches. Covenant College and Seminary, then located in St. Louis, Missouri, honored him in 1961 with the degree of Doctor of Divinity.

In 1966, Dr Young's wife died of cancer. He and his seven children returned to the United States where he completed a M. Th. degree at Calvin Seminary, writing on Christology. In 1967, he moved to Lookout Mountain, Georgia, to become Covenant College's professor of missions. The next year he married a fellow faculty member, Jane Brooks, a member of the English department.

The Connection

In 1968, I began my years as a student at Covenant College. My wife, in God's providence, who was yet unknown to me, began her studies in that same institution in 1969. We together took a course he offered called the Covenant Theology of Missions. Afterward, I took every course that was offered in the Missions/Bible Department by Dr. Young. I believe I took all the courses Dr. Young taught at that time. He had a direct approach that was softened by constant questions that he actually tried to answer from the Scripture and our doctrine, as found in the *Westminster Confession of Faith*, and *Larger* and *Shorter Catechisms*. It was impressed upon me in an indelible way that the great work God had set before His Church was not disconnected from all the rest that we believe. To find that missions was not unfounded by our whole system of doctrine was so comforting. Rather, missions had a form and foundation, warrant and wherewithal that flowed from the whole of the redemptive purpose and provision of God. At that time I did not feel, or perhaps would not admit to myself, that I had felt a call to take the gospel to the nations. I did, however, feel myself confirmed in pursuing a call to the pastoral ministry and confirmation by the church.

The Remains of the Day

Dr. Young retired in 1981, and, with their daughter, he and Jane moved to Japan to continue missionary work under the World Presbyterian Missions of which he had been president for three years. Two of his sons presently serve in Japan.

Other than this book, which was originally given as lectures and published as a series of ten pamphlets, Dr. Young has written and published, along with other booklets and articles, two books, *The Two Empires of Japan*, and *By Foot to China*. I require *The Motive and Aim of Missions* for my course Theology and Method of Missions at the Reformed Presbyterian Theological Seminary in Pittsburgh, and among other texts required for reading in my course African and Asian Indigenous Church, you will find *The Two Empires of Japan*. The testimony of Japanese students in my classes is that that book is as relevant to understanding missions in Japan today as when published in 1958.

The effect of Dr. Young's teaching upon our lives and work would be felt again. I married my wife, also named Jane, in 1970, completed seminary in 1977, and was a pastor in the middle of Pennsylvania, then in Philadelphia, and in 1993 was called to regather our scattered flock in the new little nation of Eritrea, which had just withdrawn from war-savaged Ethiopia. Missionaries from the Orthodox Presbyterian Church had labored there from 1943 to around 1977, building a well-known clinic in Ghinda, halfway between the highlands and the Red Sea, and establishing groups of believers in several locations. In 1994, the Committee on Foreign Missions of that church asked us to go and join those who had done exploratory work in the new situation and start worship there. We wrapped up our life and sold or gave away much of what we had and moved to Eritrea in that year. In just a small handful of years we rebuilt our hospital there, established a worshiping congregation in the capital city, with other outlying centers of worship, and found it necessary to leave the country, cede the hospital to the insistence of the government of Eritrea, and leave the budding church there in the hands of the young leadership and the sovereign Lord who had brought her into existence. After a short time, we were called to pastor a small rural church in Western Pennsylvania north of Pittsburgh. Within a year or so a request came that I teach the required course in missions at the Reformed Presbyterian Theological Seminary of the Reformed Presbyterian Church of North America—the same church that sponsors this publishing company. It is a great joy for me to share with students today what a Reformed Presbyterian Church Evangelical Synod missionary taught me, an Orthodox Presbyterian pastor/missionary, as I teach them in the seminary of the Reformed Presbyterian Church of North America. This has been an ecumenical experience of the best sort. This wonderful gospel of God's sovereign grace really is our common heritage. And I have experienced this firsthand.

Clear, Mild, and Gentle

In 1969, my then bride-to-be and I entered Dr. Young's course on the Covenant Theology of Missions. There we read the ten pamphlets put together as this book. There we began to have the spiritual, intellectual, and doctrinal provisions that we would need to draw upon over what is now nearly 40 years of preparing for and serving in the kingdom of God as students, seminarian and wife, then pastor and wife, missionary and wife, and pastor/professor and wife. My wife's own words are that Dr. Young, by his teaching, didn't just prepare us to be missionaries, he gave us the equipment for the "mission impossible" that foreign missions truly is. Furthermore, while listening to a gentle, mild, but clear and straightforward presentation of the biblical underpinning for missions, my wife easily embraced the "doctrines of grace" or the sovereignty of God in salvation, or, if you will, the Reformed faith.

On three counts, then, I feel that I owe Dr. Young an unrepayable debt of gratitude. First, I am thankful for Dr. Young' instruction that supplied the provision for an understanding of evangelism and missions that has been helpful and useful for my pastoral ministry in the United States, and prepared my wife to be a wonderful, suitable help, who was in full agreement with what we were doing. When I said that I was considering going to Eritrea, she immediately said yes, let's go. Then, second, when called to the mission field, having been supplied, I felt as ready as I could be for a task for which no one is adequate. The third count on which I owe Dr. Young a debt of gratitude is that when I was asked to teach the required missions course at RPTS, I was not left flat-footed in regard to what text or what written material could be assigned that would be profitable for all the students. Over recent years my students have ranged from a professor of microbiology, who is now the president of the board of RPTS, to men working in city churches who are seeking to theologically advance themselves by pursuing a formal education while already serving faithfully and full-time as pastors in those congregations. This material written by a true gentleman of the Christian faith does service for all. It is as a result of student appreciation that this volume is coming to publication—their student appreciation, and my student appreciation. Is it not the case that we always and ever remain the student? There is only one Teacher.

Approach

It was Dr. Young's conviction that a careful analysis of missions will lead to new and deeper interest in it; that such a study would not prove to be a detour from the pursuit of actually obeying the Great Commission. He was a productive man who had not succumbed to the urge of this age to ill-conceived action represented in the motto, "just do it." In an age of independent missions agencies he did not undervalue the role of the Church in missions; he taught that the Great Commission carries in itself the necessity of missions being understood as an enterprise of the organized Church as Church, led by the officers of the Church, supplied by the ordinances of the Church: the preaching of the Word of God written, the sacraments, prayer, and church discipline. While Dr. Young realized and taught that if any who heard the gospel believed, then that was most surely the Spirit of God supplying that hearing; nevertheless, he equally emphasized that it is the duty of those who proclaim the Word of God, who are set apart to that office, that they take every pain to make the gospel as full and clear as they are able.

This work does not avoid the many problems in missions. We have here in this work a discussion of elenctics, of accommodation and identification (how do we avoid compromising the integrity of the gospel?). There are such questions covered as, What shall we teach of the doctrines of the Bible? What are the marks of the indigenous church—and how do we get there from here? What is an *indigenous* church? For that matter, what is missions? In all these topics, there is a reasoned and reasonable approach squarely based on the Bible and sound Bible doctrine that provides hope for the missionary and those interested in missions, but also hope for those that we would seek, and by God's grace, find with the gospel. The unflinching assertion in the argument of these pages is for the unembarrassed presentation of, and insistence upon, the uniqueness of

Christianity. All of this is set in the context of and appreciation for the histori-cal Reformation doctrine.

This is illustrated by several of the definitions of the items referred to above. Defining things is everything, isn't it? And one is quite taken by the thoughtful definition that Dr. Young gives for missions in this work. He writes, "Missions is the work of the Triune God, through His Church, of sending Christ's ambassadors to all nations to proclaim His whole Word, for the salvation of lost men, the establishment of indigenous churches, and the coming of God's kingdom, all for the glory of God." One can see, however, the development in his thought over the years in the revision that he gave to us in class to supplement what is written here. In his revised definition of mis-sions he stated, "Missions is the work of the Triune God, moving His church in love, to send Christ's ambassadors to proclaim to the world the gospel of His covenant of life (grace) that men from all nations might be made disciples, build His Church and fulfill their covenant task, seeking to bring all things into subjection to God for the true restoration and advancement of men and the glory of God."

Also, in this work, one isn't left wondering what it is toward which the mis-sionary labors. Ultimately, it is the glory of God. Penultimately, looking toward that for which we strive in order to achieve our ultimate goal, we are here given a target to shoot for. It is the indigenous church as defined in this way: "Thus an indigenous church is considered here to be a body of believers organized for worship, the edification of the saints, and the spread of the gospel, planted in a soil foreign to the gospel until the arrival of missionaries through whose labors a native church was produced, founded upon Jesus Christ as He is offered in the Scriptures, sharing the life of the land, self-governing, self-supporting, and self-propagating from devotion to Christ, and aiming at the extension of His kingdom."

Of course, one of the thorniest problems in missions and the establish-ment of indigenous churches is the matter of support, and the end of support for the struggling self-supporting indigenous church. When and how does aid stop? Dr. Young looks at that with a clear eye. That eye is not jaundiced, how-ever, by skepticism or cynicism. His approach looks in faith to the Provider. The last sentence of the book after dealing with this particular topic perhaps introduces the whole work best. So I leave you to start your reading with the positive and encouraging words Dr. Young uses to close the book, "God's work, done by God's men, in God's way, will have God's support." Now read on. This is where he would take you.

—*Steven F. Miller,*
pastor, adjunct professor of missions at RPTS
RoseMerry Croft
April 3, 2007

Introduction

While there have been great victories in the missionary conquests of the church of Christ, there have also been great tragedies. Among some peoples and in some centers, the work of the gospel has been set back years and generations by those who wished most to promote it. We refer not to the false brethren who, by apostasy of life and doctrine, do great harm to the cause of Christ, but to many whom we would not hesitate to call true believers.

In this series of studies, Dr. John M. L. Young helps us to review our "Mission to the Nations" and to seek out afresh the true incentive, basis, foundation, aim, and method of Christian witness to the world. For indeed, almost every failure on the mission field can be traced to an aim, a motive, an incentive, a method, or a doctrine that was not founded on the written Word of God.

We remember well a sage missionary's advice before we went to the mission field ourselves: "Don't go to the field until you are sure you know why you are going; and you are never sure of a thing until you can put it down in black and white and truly believe it." In these studies, Dr. Young has done us a great service in ably guiding us by putting down in black and white the only true theology of foreign missions. We can believe it, because it is the theology of the Word of God as it relates to the Great Commission.

For those of you who do not know Dr. Young, he is at present a missionary under World Presbyterian Missions in Japan and the president of the Japan Christian Theological Seminary in Tokyo. Dr. Young has served on three mission fields—namely, China, Manchuria, and Japan—and was the son of missionary parents. Jonathan Goforth of China was instrumental in Dr. Young's call to the mission field.

These pamphlets were originally a series of lectures delivered by Dr. Young at Covenant College and Seminary, St. Louis, Mo., where they were enthusiastically received by both students and faculty. Dr. Young is a graduate of Acadia University in Nova Scotia, and Faith Theological Seminary, then in Wilmington, Del. He has done postgraduate work at Calvin Seminary in Grand Rapids, Mich., and was awarded a Doctor of Divinity degree by Covenant College and Seminary, St. Louis, Mo.

—*William A. Mahlow*
General Secretary, World Presbyterian Missions, Inc.
October 19, 1962

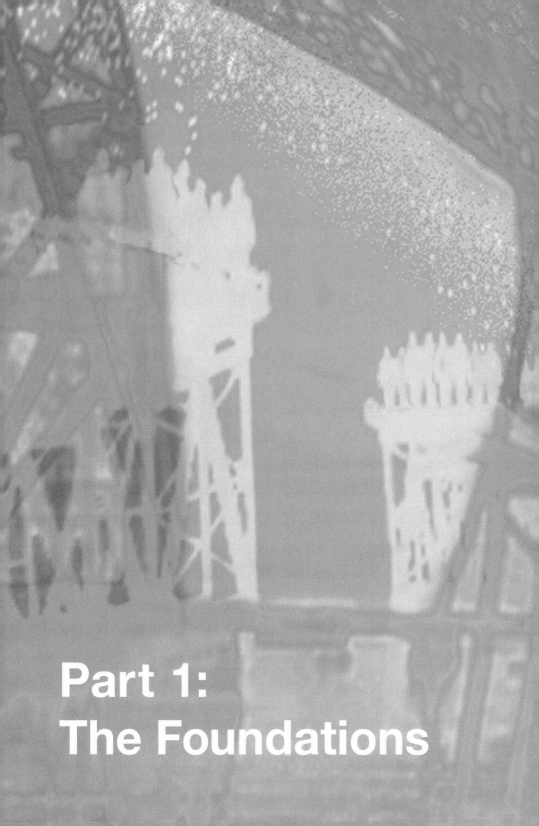

Part 1:
The Foundations

The Basis of Missions

"As the love of God, from God's side, is the motive in His Son's mission to earth and the glory of God His aim, so too, reciprocally, from man's side the love of God must be the motive of missionary effort and the glory of God the aim."

W hat do we mean by *missions*? If we are to discuss its basis, certainly we will have to define what we mean by the term. As we shall be using it here, missions is the work of the Triune God, through His Church, of sending Christ's ambassadors to all nations to proclaim His whole Word for the salvation of lost men, the establishment of in-digenous churches,* and the coming of God's kingdom, all for the glory of God. This definition encompasses, as we shall shortly observe, the first three petitions of the prayer our Lord directed us to pray. Just as a stone splashed into a pool sends its ripples out in ever-expanding concentric circles to the distant borders,

---

* By *indigenous church in the missionary context* is meant, as defined in a later chapter, a church planted in a soil foreign to the gospel, until the arrival of missionaries through whose labors a native church is produced, founded upon Jesus Christ as He is offered in the Scriptures, sharing the life of the land, self-governing, self-supporting, and self-propagat-ing from devotion to Christ, and aiming at the extension of His kingdom.

so we envisage in this definition the work of Christ starting at a center and spreading outwards to its furthest goal. True missions, thus, have their source in God, their work undertaken by men of His choosing, and their goal in the worldwide advancement of His cause for His glory.

Missions, as we use the term here, has thus to do primarily with foreign missions, the work of God's people in sending forth His servants to take the gospel to other nations where it is unknown or little known. We think of the work of spreading the gospel to one's own people as evangelism—the home task of the Church whether in the area of the local church or to other communities in the nation. When an indigenous church is established abroad, it likewise does not send out missionaries to its own people, but evangelists to preach the gospel to them. The work of pursuing those who have left the fold of the church, or covenant children who have grown up indifferent to it, is but one phase of evangelism (certainly not its entire operation, as has been held by some). We do not insist on this distinction of terminology, but we do believe that it is a convenient differentiation and one that has considerable traditional usage behind it.

In considering the true basis on which this foreign missionary effort should rest, we are, I believe, primarily concerned with the basic motive and aim of missionary endeavors. These two words, *motive* and *aim*, are not synonymous, although sometimes in every day speech we may use them that way. A man's motive has to do with that which is within him, that which moves him to action, an emotion or desire operating on his will giving him an incentive to action. One's aim, on the other hand, is without him; it is the object to be obtained. The motive is the stimulus moving one to try to attain his aim.

The foreign missionary enterprise has been going on for a long time. Why should we now begin to inquire into its true motive and aim? some may ask. If theologians begin to theorize about what the Church has been practicing for many generations, is it not a sign of decadence, of turning from good works to mere words? We have our commandment to preach the gospel to the whole world. Why don't we get on with the job of doing it and stirring up interest in it, instead of inquiring into the "why's" and "what's" of it, they say. But such reasoning is shortsighted as it rests on an unnecessary antithesis, that is, that careful analysis of missions will not lead to a new and deeper interest in it.

We may indeed be thankful that the Church has been sending out the gospel to foreign fields for a long time. Our hearts, however, may also be saddened by the knowledge of many a tragedy because these inquiries into proper motives and right aims were not carefully made before the missionary task was undertaken. We are saddened, for instance, at the result when those whose motive was to help reach multitudes in heathen lands, whom they erroneously thought to be hungering for Christ, and who gave up in frustration and despair when they realized this was not so, but that the heathen were more apt to scoff at the idea of a crucified Savior. We are saddened also by the haphazard wanderings, unorganized efforts, wasted attempts, and final discouragement and defeat of others who had no clear understanding of what their real aim was.

What should be their aim? To preach the gospel, of course. But should it be merely to present it and pass on? Or should they stay longer, endeavoring to lead interested ones into a deeper understanding and a real conversion? Or should they perhaps stay still longer until an indigenous church is formed? Or should they stay even longer, until the new church is establishing other churches and training a native ministry to reach out to distant places for the expansion of Christ's kingdom? Which of these is the real missionary aim and the fulfillment of the Lord's commission? The foreign missionary enterprise has too many illustrations of defeated missionaries and wrecked missionary efforts because the true basis of missions, its real motive and aim, was not correctly apprehended. What then should the Church consider to be its true motive and aim for missions?

Historical Models

Let us inquire first how the church through the years has construed its own missionary motive and aim. A wide range of answers have been given, the activity fluctuations revealed in the study of the history of missions being determined to a great extent by the differing missionary motives and aims of various periods. The history of missions seems to reveal a fluctuation from warmth to coolness, from zeal to relative indifference, corresponding to the soundness of the missionary motives and aims of the period. The pendulum swung slowly from one side to the other: when the ever-present tendency of Christians and their churches to be engulfed by worldly motives and aims predominated, eventually a reaction would begin in some area of Christ's Church, turning at least one segment back to her true calling. This was the hand of God ensuring that His plan for the world—that every nation should hear His gospel and some from every tribe and tongue come under His dominion, into His kingdom—should not fail.

The first century Christians were joyful lay preachers. They went everywhere preaching the gospel (Acts 4:8) with hearts full of love and gratitude for their great salvation, desiring to tell their good news to others that they too might experience it. Who of us has not felt the natural and spontaneous desire to tell others some good news that has filled our hearts with joy? This seems indeed the spirit with which the early Christians witnessed the good news, or God's reconciliation through Christ. It was accompanied by a sense of urgency springing from the realization that this was the day of salvation, a day shortened by the briefness of life and the soon return of Jesus.

But as the centuries passed and the pagan empire, which had so resisted the gospel, professed the Christian faith, and then had its prerogatives assumed by the leaders of a church engulfed by worldly ambition and pride, the motives became changed. Increasingly, the motivation through the medieval ages seems to have been a desire to spread the glory of the Church, aiming at extending her political and religious dominion ever to more distant regions. Military conquests and discoveries of new lands were viewed as victories for Christianity in opening doors for the establishing of a Christian culture. The missionary enterprise thus became entangled with this whole concept of political conquest, of Christianizing the heathen by getting them to conform to the cultural standards of the mother country, and of subduing newly discovered lands with the Christianization process in order that economically profitable trade could be carried on with them.

Even after the Reformation we find these mixed motives continuing, through the efforts of the great trading companies of the Protestant countries. The Dutch East India Company, for instance, sent chaplains to the East Indies and offered them a bonus of a guilder for each native baptized. One can at least acknowledge the insight of these businessmen in perceiving the beneficial effects to trade that the conversion of the heathen would bring, an insight woefully lacking in most foreign traders abroad today, even though we may deprecate their method of stimulating the missionary effort by appealing to the profit motive of the chaplains!

But with the Reformation the reaction began to set in, and the pendulum began to swing the other way. The Reformation turned the minds of God's people back to Christ and His Word. In the late 17th century, we find the Moravian Brethren shaking free from the concept of a state church trying to spread Christianity from political or economic motives, or endeavoring to Christianize the natives through the implanting of their Western culture. Theirs was more of the first century spirit—in devotion to Christ going out to tell lost men of the salvation that was in Christ. It has been estimated that within two decades they established more missionary outposts than the Protestant state churches of the previous two centuries. The missionary tradition that they set was again marked by a sense of urgency, both because of the shortness of life and the impending return of Christ.

In Holland, one Reformed theologian of the mid-17th century summed up the aims of missions in a noble way. Voetius, in his work on church polity, undertook a careful consideration of missions, presenting the aim as being threefold: (1) the conversion of the heathen, (2) the founding of the church, and (3) the glory and manifestation of divine grace. In spite of this splendid presentation and the later work of the Moravians, the Protestant churches as a whole did relatively little by way of foreign missions, and the 17th century closed in a growing tide of life-killing rationalism. The spiritual awakenings in England and America in the 19th century, however, stirred anew the love for Christ and zeal to spread His gospel to the uttermost parts. The greatest missionary effort in the history of Christianity began. Sometimes the motive was stated as being the love of Christ; at others, the emphasis was put on the duty of obeying His command, or compassion for the lost, or the desire to help those in darkness share in the great light of modern civilization and progress. For most, the aim was thus extended beyond the immediate objective of seeing souls saved to seeing them educated as well as seeing churches established and native ministers trained.

But again the pendulum swung, and under the influence of the age of Darwin and the ultimacy of modern science, modernist unbelief chilled the churches. The motive of missions in these churches was man-centered; philanthropic (to relieve human suffering), and intellectual (to bring modem learning). The hope was that through these means, and the teaching of Christian standards of morality, good, civilized societies would be formed, resting on principles of justice and love. The establishment of such man-improved societies, through the preaching and practice of the "social gospel," was equated with the building of the kingdom of God. The emphasis was on service and education to improve religions, not to convert from them. Great sums of money were spent on the institutional work of high schools, universities, and hospitals. The advent of two world wars, however, and the savagery of the educated men they revealed, has done much to discredit this motive and aim.

Today, again a reaction has set in against all of this and the pendulum is swinging the other way. Again, the hand of God is stirring His people, and His Church is turning to missionary endeavor in perhaps its greatest effort in history. Young hearts are being challenged. With what motives should they be moved? What should be the aims they seek to accomplish? How should we, as those who hold to the Reformed faith in the mid-20th century, construe the motives and aims on which the missionary enterprise should be based?

Christ's Love

Let us now consider our conception of the motives and aims of missions. Our answer, as those who hold the Reformed faith, must come from the Bible. If we consider the world from the point of view of its present condition—the fallen, sinful, depraved world under the condemnation of death, the world into which the first man was born, a subsequent murderer—and if we ask, "What was God's attitude towards it?" the Bible gives us a clear answer. From the words of our Lord Himself, in one of our most precious texts, we obtain the answer. "For God so loved the world, that he gave his only begotten Son, that whosoever believeth in him should not perish, but have everlasting life" (John 3:16).

Ultimately, from God's side, the motive behind His Son's mission was the love of God, and the aim was the glory of God. It was the world of sinful men that God loved, and this love that moved Him to send His Son. It could not be stated more clearly nor more beautifully than in the words of John 3:16: "For God so loved the world . . . ." It was God's good pleasure to win back to Himself a world He could easily and justly destroy for its wicked rebellion and sin. But "in this was manifested the love of God towards us, because that God sent his only begotten Son into the world, that we might live through him" (1 John 4:9). He was moved by love to reveal His love.

There is no higher objective than the glory of God, but what do we mean when we speak of this as being God's aim in sending His Son? When we say the glory of God is the goal in John 3:16, we have indeed expanded the aim cited there, that men might be saved. This is justified not only by the fact that all of God's works are for His glory, but also because of our Lord's own description of the manner in which His coming to earth glorified His Father, in His high priestly prayer. John 17:4 and the following verses mentions three specifics in which His coming glorified the Father.

In verse 4 He said He finished the work given Him to do. What did He do? He replies: "I do always those things that please him" (John 8:29). "I seek not mine own will, but the will of the Father which hath sent me" (John 5:30). His taking of the cup was the will of God and He yielded to that will, saying, "not my will, but thine, be done" (Luke 22:42). His fulfilling of the will of God was His claim to have glorified God.

Again, in verse 7 and following, God is glorified when men are caused to know that what the Son has He has received from the Father, and that the authority and Lordship of the Son are the dominion and sovereignty of God. God is glorified when the men He has given to the Son are sent forth into the world to preach the gospel with Christ's authority (17:18) and when others believe on Him as the Word is proclaimed, and, thus, when the world learns than the Father has sent the Son (John 20:21). God is glorified as the Son's disciples go into the world to tell of the Father's love, that men throughout the world might believe on Him and be drawn into His one fold. God is glorified, in other words, as His ambassadors are sent to proclaim His Word to the world and men believe and enter His kingdom.

Finally, our Lord concludes His prayer in verse 26 with the emphatic reiteration (v. 6) that He has declared the name of God. Throughout the history of Israel, the exaltation of the name of God was associated with His glory. In Psalm 8:1 we read: "O Lord our Lord, how excellent is thy name in all the earth! who hast set thy glory above the heavens." In Psalm 79:9 the psalmist cries: "Help us, O God of our salvation, for the glory of thy name: and deliver us, and purge away our sins, for thy name's sake." Psalm 148:13 declares: "Let them praise the name of the Lord; for his name alone is excellent; his glory is above the earth and heaven." Psalm 72:19 has the world in view: "And blessed be his glorious name for ever: and let the whole earth be filled with his glory; Amen, and Amen."

In John 12:27-28 Jesus cries: "Now is my soul troubled; and what shall I say?

Father, save me from this hour: but for this cause came I unto this hour. Father, glorify thy name. Then came there a voice from heaven, saying, 'I have both glorified it, and will glorify it again.'" The Father speaks from heaven of His purpose to glorify His name. He who magnifies the name of God glorifies Him. Jesus attests His declaration and manifestation of that name to the world—of what it means to be God—as evidence that He had glorified the Father.

Our Lord submitted three aspects of His work in prayer as attesting that He had glorified God: the fulfillment of His work, the magnification of His name, and the sending forth of proclaimers of His Word who would extend His kingdom to cover all in the world the Father had given Him. These three, although in a different order, are the same as the first three petitions in our Lord's model prayer. We are told to pray for, and assuredly the assumption is to work for also, the magnification of God's name, the coming of His kingdom and the fulfilling of His will on earth.

The Old Testament saints had a holy reverence for the name of God and deep concern that it not be dishonored among the nations. As far as their general attitude towards the heathen was concerned, however, this seemed to be the extent of their concern: that they would not cause the name of God to be blasphemed among the heathen and that His name would be glorified among them. The thought of a further concern, of compassion for the lost state of the heathen, seems scarcely to appear in their thinking, except in the message of the prophets as a future event. This great plan and eternal purpose of God was still a mystery, as Paul points out in Ephesians 3:3-6. That mystery, however, is revealed to us, and we must therefore pray and work, as long as we are on this earth, for the magnification of His precious name among all nations, with our eyes of faith looking forward to the coming of that day when some shall be redeemed "to God by thy blood out of every kindred, and tongue, and people, and nation" (Rev. 5:9).

In the second petition of the Lord's prayer, we pray, "Thy Kingdom come." The Old Testament saints, apart from some notable exceptions, apparently had little realization of the role human proclamation would have in the work of making God's name glorious among the nations and extending His kingdom. They were told by the prophets, however, that God's light would reach the Gentiles at some future date and that God's kingdom would some day be a world dominion.

And he said, It is a light thing that thou shouldest be my servant to raise up the tribes of Jacob, and to restore the preserved of Israel: I will also give thee for a light to the Gentiles, that thou mayest be my salvation unto the end of the earth. (Isa. 49:6)

Arise, shine; for thy light is come, and the glory of the Lord is risen upon thee. For, behold, the darkness shall cover the earth, and gross darkness the people: but the Lord shall arise upon thee, and his glory shall be seen upon thee. And the Gentiles shall come to thy light, and kings to the brightness of thy rising. (Isa. 60:1-3)

All the ends of the world shall remember and turn unto the Lord: and all the kindreds of the nations shall worship before thee. For the kingdom is the Lord's: and he is the governor among the nations. (Ps. 22:27-28)

I saw in the night visions, and, behold, one like the Son of man came with the clouds of heaven, and came to the Ancient of days, and they brought him near before him. And there was given him dominion, and glory, and a kingdom, that all people, nations, and languages, should serve him: his dominion is an everlasting dominion, which shall not pass away, and his kingdom that which shall not be destroyed. (Dan. 7:13-14)

Rejoice greatly, O daughter of Zion; shout, O daughter of Jerusalem: behold, thy King cometh unto thee: he is just, and having salvation; lowly, and riding upon an ass, and upon a colt the foal of an ass. And I will cut off the chariot from Ephraim, and the horse from Jerusalem, and the battle bow shall be cut off: and he shall speak peace unto the heathen: and his dominion shall be from sea even to sea, and from the river even to the ends of the earth. (Zech. 9:9-10)

It was the New Testament revelation that first clearly associated the extension of God's kingdom with widespread preaching by God's people. Both Matthew and Luke show how Jesus began His ministry by preaching about the kingdom (Matt. 4:17; Luke 4:43). "I must preach the kingdom of God to other cities also: for therefore am I sent." In the great Olivet discourse he declared, "And this gospel of the kingdom shall be preached in all the world for a witness unto all nations; and then shall the end come" (Matt. 24:14). In the last verse of Acts, Luke summarizes the preaching of Paul in Rome by saying that he was there "preaching the kingdom of God, and teaching those things which concern the Lord Jesus Christ, with all confidence" (Acts 28:31).

The New Testament made it clear that there was an aspect in which the fulfillment of the prayer "Thy Kingdom come" was related to the activity of men and activity of the Church. Not until that work was done would the King return to earth in power and great glory to reign over His kingdom in bodily presence. That work of the Church was to preach the gospel of the kingdom to every nation, tribe and tongue—the missionary enterprise! By the missionary effort of the Church, would the authority and power, the dominion and kingdom of Christ be extended into all the world. The worldwide missionary effort of the Church must be carried out for the fulfillment of the prayer, "Thy Kingdom come."

This becomes clear too in the way our Lord introduces His Great Commission in Matthew 28:18: "All power is given unto me in heaven and in earth. Go ye therefore, and teach all nations." All authority is Christ's. He is no usurper! It is rightfully His because it was given Him by the Father! We are to go forth to tell men of every nation, and to seek to win them to acknowledge His rule, His lordship. His is the dominion and His the kingdom, even though, in this age, a usurper prince has stolen the affections of the people and is leading them in rebellion against their rightful King. Now the true King calls upon His servants to become His good soldiers, to go forth to all nations with His gospel to oppose Satan and preach peace and deliverance from the bondage of the false prince and his power, to endeavor to bring men back to the dominion of the rightful King, into the kingdom of God. This is our calling, the task of Christ's Church for this age. For this, we as Christians and the Church as instituted were brought into existence to be a holy people unceasing in witness to the Holy God. We are to bend every effort, expend every energy, and make every sacrifice for the spread of the gospel to every nation and tongue, the conversion of the heathen, the establishment of churches, and the extension of God's kingdom. This calling and work of His Church must go on until the task is done, until every tribe has heard and some from every tongue are saved as trophies of His grace (Matt. 24:14; Rev. 5:9). This must be our goal if we are to be faithful Christians and the faithful Church.

Our utmost effort in this missionary enterprise will hasten the work to its conclusion and hasten the coming of the day of the King's triumphal return to earth. Is this not the probable meaning of 2 Peter 3:12, "Looking for and hastening the coming of the day of God"? We cannot change the appointed day, but our work is necessary as the appointed means to fulfill the requirement to take the gospel to all His elect before He returns. This task God does not do directly, nor is it appointed to the angels to do it, but to men, to those whom He has redeemed, to His Church, to us (Eph. 3:10). The day of its fulfillment will be the day of His return as the restored King of all the earth, reigning in personal presence, with every knee bending to His authority and dominion, as the acknowledged supreme sovereign and Lord. Then, finally, shall come the moment when He will return the kingdom He has won with His blood and Word, to His Father (1 Cor. 15:24-26). Here is the plan of God for this age. Here is His aim and our aim: that He shall be glorified before all the world and above all. Here is His motive of love revealed in that He seeks to win back that which He could righteously destroy: "For God so loved the world, that he gave his only begotten Son . . . that the world through him might be saved" (John 3:16-17).

When we pray "Thy Kingdom come," we pray for the extension of the knowledge of that wonderful love to all the world, that men might be brought under its sway and His dominion. We are praying that men will go tell the heathen nations of His glorious redeeming name of Father, Son, and Holy Spirit.

The second petition of the Lord's prayer, like the first, is thus a missionary petition. To work for the fulfillment of this prayer—to take the gospel to all nations—is to do the work of God; and our Lord in His high priestly prayer indicated that to do God's work is to glorify Him. The missionary effort is wholeheartedly engaged in that work, and its basic aim is thus supremely the glory of God.

The third petition of the Lord's prayer likewise has definite missionary implications, since it is His will that the gospel be preached in all the world and that men submit to His dominion in every nation. "Thy will be done in earth as it is in heaven" certainly includes the petition that the desire to do God's will should increase among men until it exists in all the earth. The problem of the secret, unrevealed will of God, of course, is involved here. We do not know the secret will of God concerning how many men, and in what nations, shall turn to doing God's will in any given period in the future; but we do know about the revealed will of God "who will have all men to be saved, and to come unto the knowledge of the truth" (1 Tim. 2:4). In the third petition we pray for the fulfillment of the will of God, and we know that this does include the constant spreading of the desire among men to do God's will until it reaches every nation and until there are some out of every tongue on earth who have yielded to the will of God.

These three petitions that our Lord taught us to pray coincide with the three evidences He submitted in His high priestly prayer as demonstrating that His life on earth had been lived for the glory of God: the doing of God's will, the sending out of men into the world with the message of His kingdom, and the manifestation of His hallowed name. To do these things is to glorify God. Christ accomplished them in order to glorify God. God so loved the world that He sent His Son to accomplish them. The aim of God then was His glory, even as His motive was His love. Our Lord has asked us to make them our aim too by praying for them.

As the love of God, from God's side, is the motive in His Son's mission to earth and the glory of God His aim, so too, reciprocally, from man's side, the love of God must be the motive of missionary effort, and the glory of God the aim.

When we say our basic motive in missions is the love of God, we are on solidly scriptural grounds. When Paul cites the motive, which drove him on in spite of all opposition and terrible persecutions to take the gospel to the heathen, he does not refer to the commandment, the Great Commission, to go to the nations with the gospel. It is his aim to fulfill that commandment, but his motive for doing so is his loving gratitude for the mercy of God that He has experienced. He refers to this in 2 Corinthians 4:1: "Therefore seeing we have this ministry, as we have received mercy, we faint not." He did not quit in spite of the many persecutions and calamities listed in 2 Corinthians 11 because of the mercy of God to him. He reiterates this in 2 Corinthians 5:13-14: "For whether we be beside ourselves, it is to God: or whether we be sober, it is for your cause. For the *love of Christ* constraineth us." However we construe the genitive (possessive) here, the meaning is clear. We love Him because He first loved us. His implanted love brings our reciprocal love. And this, in turn, causes us to love what He loves, to desire what He desires, to work for that which He worked. In loving gratitude for His mercy and love to us, we want to take the news of that loving mercy to those for whom He came. The establishment of the God-ward vertical relation of love is the necessary basis for the horizontal man-ward one. Compassion for the lost state of men and desire to see them saved are thus noble motives and aims, though subsidiary to and derived from the loftiest of all—the love of God and the glory of God.

The twofold summary of the Ten Commandments reveals this also. First comes the love of God, with all our heart, mind, and soul; then follows the necessity of loving our neighbor as ourselves, for our Savior has loved him and called upon us to love him for His sake. This implanted love of God alone is sufficient to provide the outgoing love necessary to produce and sustain the obedience, zeal, perseverance, devotion, and compassion to carry on the missionary enterprise.

It is the inner constraining love of Christ that stirs us to compassion for the lost. We see their need, as lost without a Shepherd, as Christ did when He was moved with compassion for them (Matt. 9:36-38), because of His implanted love. This compassion is more than sympathy for physical distress, poverty, or disease, although it is this also. It is a compassion moved by these but that sees the real need as deeper: a spiritual darkness and superstition that blinds the heart and holds its victim in the bondage of sin and under the condemnation of hell.

Yet not infrequently, it is the physical plight of lost men that first moves our compassion and stirs us to help them. As a high school boy in Japan before the war, I went with a visiting missionary from Korea to visit a Korean area of the great city of Osaka. There were more than 500,000 Koreans living in that city then, more than in any city in Korea except the capital, Seoul. Many of them were young men who had come over to find work, but few had. The great majority lived in conditions of abject poverty. We had heard that many had become victims of the morphine habit and thus were hopeless drug addicts. After the Sunday morning service in a small church, some of the members took us through a large lumberyard and down small alleys where I saw some of the most miserable people I had ever seen. There were scores of young men sitting along the gutters of the alleys, their arms and legs covered with the marks of the injection needles and in some places infected. Many of them were lying in the hot sun in a complete stupor, and all of them were in rags.

Nothing I have ever seen in a lifetime in the Orient seems so completely to symbolize the meaning of the word "lost" as did those poor wretches. Utterly, hopelessly lost! They had no life for the present and no hope for the future. They were only living to steal something from a backyard or a front door to get enough money to buy more morphine to inject into their dirty, pockmarked bodies, in order to pass out into the oblivion of the marvelous dreams of paradise the drug was supposed to make possible. Slaves of sin and death, they were trying to escape the reality of their terrible lives by drugging their minds and seeking to live in a dream world. We witnessed to many of them, but they seemed to have so destroyed themselves and corroded their wills that they had thoughts for nothing other than the satisfaction of the fleshly craving they had brought on themselves. It is a picture I have never gotten out of my mind. Later that year Dr. Jonathan Goforth, the great missionary to Manchuria, visited our home, and we had frequent talks about the Orient's need. I felt that the Lord would have me return to the Far East with His gospel, the power of God unto salvation, to a people whose invisible souls, without Christ, were just as lost as those poor men who were so visibly perishing in the slums of Osaka.

It is the loving mercy of Christ, manifested to us, which enables us to see this need and to be concerned to alleviate it, to help them by bringing them into Christ's fold under His dominion and deliverance. Our missionary motivation must be Christ's love, Christ-implanted and Christ-constrained.

God's Glory

Our aim as the glory of God in the missionary enterprise is, first of all, the same aim stated to be that of God in sending His Son, that is, the salvation of the lost and the conversion of the heathen. The vision and outreaching effort of every Christian and every church must embrace this as a basic goal: to work for the preaching of the gospel to the nations of the world if they are to be faithful. This is God's aim for His glory and must be ours. Here the missionary enterprise must start: the home churches sending preachers to the heathen and the preachers beginning by seeking to win heathen to Christ, to bring them into His fold.

But secondly, following this start, the aim of the missionary and of the sending churches must be to establish among the heathen indigenous churches with the converts. We will be dealing with these aims again so here all that is necessary is to emphasize the following. Our Lord declared that He would build His Church on the true, apostolic confession of Himself, and the effort of His apostles to establish churches wherever converts were made was Christ's work of building His Church as He promised. So must that effort be ours too as we preach, if we are to be the heirs of the apostles and the faithful servants of Christ. The Church is the Christian unit provided by Christ, for the edification of the saints (within) and the reaching of the world of the unconverted (without) with the gospel.

As the churches are planted on the mission field, if they are to grow and do the work of Christ's churches, they must be rooted in the people, the members providing for their own church, doing God's work themselves for His glory; in other words, they must be truly indigenous churches. They must be conscious of their need not to be provided for but to provide for the gospel's spread.

Extending Christ's kingdom to their heathen compatriots must be the aim of the native church. As they do this as indigenous churches, many of the former barriers of Satan will be broken down and a much more favorable atmosphere for the extension of the gospel will prevail. The light of the gospel will dispel much of primitive paganism. The lot of man, and especially of woman, will improve. Christianity inevitably elevates the standards of society, while a diminishing of the Christian witness conversely restores the acceptability of moral laxness. But progress never will mean that the battle with Satan is over! Social enlightenment is not conversion of the soul. Spiritual enlightenment must stem from soul renewal, Holy Spirit regeneration. Modern prosperity often brings spiritual indifference, a new barrier. New, sophisticated interpretations of the old religions arise; and nationalism or communist conquests bring new satanic barriers. The struggle goes on. If we are to be victors then, we must keep our feet solidly on the Rock, Christ Jesus, motivated by the love of God and ever aiming at His eternal glory.

Questions for Study and Discussion

1. What do we mean by "missions"?
2. Why should we inquire into the true aim and motive of the missionary enterprise?
3. Name and discuss some false motives for missions, giving historical examples of the same.
4. What is the true motive for missions?
5. What is the true aim of missions?

6. How did God the Son glorify God the Father as reflected in our Lord's high priestly prayer in John 17?
7. How does this harmonize with the model prayer, which our Lord taught His Church?
8. As God progressively reveals Himself and His purpose in Scripture, what aspect of missions is emphasized in the New Testament, which is not emphasized as much in the Old Testament? What aspect of missions is emphasized in both Old and New Testaments?
9. Give the missionary implications of the first three petitions of the Lord's Prayer.
10. How does the twofold summary of the Ten Commandments, which Jesus gave, reflect the true motive for missions?

2

"We do not begin our witness to them in a void, but with the knowledge God has already spoken to them and is speaking to them."

The Presuppositions of Missions

In considering the subject of the presuppositions of missions, we are going beyond the theme of its basis, motivated by the love of God and aiming at His glory, to a consideration of the necessity for, and possibility of, a missionary enterprise. What is the nature of man that we presuppose when we speak of his need to be saved? Is man capable of being reached?

This question is asked sometimes concerning particular classes of men, such as the dedicated communists or lifelong idolaters. Are they capable of being reached? It would be foolish to send missionaries to them if they were incapable of even being contacted with the gospel. But is there a remedy powerful enough to penetrate their dark hearts and translate them into God's marvelous kingdom of light? With what presuppositions concerning these things do we face the missionary task?

Basically there are two: the condition of man as lost and the power of Christ to save. We will begin with a consideration of the condition of man as lost.

The Condition of Man as Lost

To face the missionary task realistically is of the utmost importance. Aware of what lies before us, we must be neither overly optimistic as to what we can expect, nor become pessimistic because of the hardness of the pagan heart. We need to have a clear realization of the nature of man before we go forth.

Men, whether Stone Age savages in the jungles of New Guinea or uneducated primitives in the mountains of Peru or atheistic communists in the universities of Japan, are all created in the image of God. This is the great fact of anthropology: that all men are human beings, however primitive or savage they may seem, that all have souls as well as bodies, and that all are created in God's image.

But another great fact of anthropology, a tragic fact, is that man has fallen, and in the fall the divine image was seriously marred. In some aspects, it was lost. Man lost moral excellence, righteousness, and holiness, and true knowledge as well. He needs to be supernaturally renewed in these aspects of the image of God if he is to be restored to the family of God. But having lost these, he is at enmity with God (Rom. 5:9-10), spiritually dead (Eph. 2:1) so that he has no inclination to worship the true God, and morally depraved so that he lives for the creaturely self and not for God's standards (Rom. 1:28).

Because of his sinful condition, he is under the wrath and curse of God, condemned to die physically in this life and eternally in hell (John. 3:3; Matt. 25:41). This is the perishing condition of lost men as the Bible portrays it to us.

But not all aspects of the image of God were lost in the fall. Man is the creature who is the image bearer of God. If he had completely lost that image in the fall he would no longer be man. The fall, however, did not make him "not a man." The natural man is still God's image bearer in three aspects.

First, he is a rational being with self-consciousness, having a reasonable soul that attests to him that he is more than his body. There is an ego, an inner self within him that can control his mind and is really he. His age-old and universal hope of immortality is not that his body will escape death but that his soul will.

Second, he is also a religious being with God-consciousness, having within himself ineradicably a sense of God, a *sensus deitatus*. It is this to which Paul is referring in Romans 1:19-20. "Because that which may be known of God is manifest in them; for God hath shewed it unto them. For the invisible things of him from the creation of the world are clearly seen, being understood by the things that are made, even his eternal power and Godhead; so that they are without excuse." In verse 19, we read "known." In what sense is it known? It is not a content of knowledge about God natural to all men, but an awareness that God exists. It is this basic sense, rooted into his being at his creation, that enables him to see the general revelation of God in the works of nature, including himself, for he does see it, Paul says in verse 20. He sees both that there exists a deity and an eternal power above this created world; and then, as we shall observe shortly, he sinfully suppresses this truth. This is the basis of his inexcusableness before God.

Third, man is also a responsible being with moral consciousness. Paul refers to this in Romans 2:14-15. "For when the Gentiles, which have not the law, do by nature the things contained in the law, these, having not the law are a law unto themselves; which shew the work of the law written in their hearts, their conscience also bearing witness, and their thoughts then meanwhile accusing or else excusing one another." What is man's conscience? Is it not his consciousness that he ought to do right and ought not to do wrong? This is implanted in all men, making them moral creatures and distinguishing them from the animals. It is not that the heathen innately know correctly what is right and what is wrong. The heathen have all kinds of erroneous moral standards. But they do have standards, and a conscience that tells them they ought to do what they believe to be right and ought to abstain from what they hold to be wrong. They even acknowledge that gross evil is deserving of punishment, Paul says in Romans 1:32, but they suppress this voice and go on in sin.

In this we see also the nature of unbelief. It is the nature of man's unbelieving condition to suppress all truth that would point him to God. In Romans 1:18 the Greek verb for "hold" has a prefix meaning to "hold down," or "to restrain." Men suppress the knowledge of God within them; they do not want to respond to His revelation of Himself in Nature. This revelation will never lead the heathen to God because of the sinful reaction of unbelief causing them to suppress truth pointing to God.

Yet the revelation is there, and the God-consciousness is universally in man. Paul took advantage of this in Athens when he began his sermon with a reference to their altar to the "Unknown God." There is no known instance where it has been established that a group of men have had no knowledge of God. In Manchuria in 1940, I made a missionary trip back into the northeastern mountains where conditions were very primitive. We had taken our bicycles on the train, had gotten off about 100 miles to the east of Harbin, and had ridden north. The Japanese who occupied the country at that time did not go into that area but stayed along the railway, fearing gorilla attacks. I recall on one occasion a Chinese farmer asking if I was Japanese. They had seen neither Japanese nor white men back there. We sold gospel portions, gave out tracts and witnessed of God and His salvation through Christ. Sometimes I would ask whom they worshiped, and usually they would point to some pagan temple where nature gods were worshiped. When I asked if they did not believe there was some God who was far above and superior to all these, inevitably they would reply that there was such a one, Lao Tien Yeh, the Venerable Heavenly One. But when I asked if they worshiped Him, they usually looked from one to the other, shook their heads, and admitted that they did not. The consciousness of a supreme deity was not foreign to them, but this they set aside, and worshiped and served the creature rather than the Creator.

The moral-consciousness is present in men also. Quite vivid in my memory are the many Sunday nights I sat down with a group of young Japanese university students in Tokyo with an open Bible. They were youths of keen intelligence, but all of them espoused the Marxist ideology. On a number of occasions we studied what Paul had to say in Romans 1. On one such night, the question came up as to who set the standards of right and wrong. Their consensus was that these were made by human convention, but that basically, that which speeded the cause of socialism was good and that which impeded its progress was evil. Endeavoring to make them take a more personal view of it, I asked them if they cheated on their exams. Looking somewhat sheepish, they all admitted that they did. They defended it on the basis that everyone did and that it hastened them on their way into the world and the struggle for the conquest of socialism!

Coming home that night, my thoughts were not happy ones. Could it be possible that these godless youths had succeeded in eradicating the image of God from them? Was it really gone? Yet in my heart I knew this was not possible. Then one of the young women in the class, who was riding the train part way with me, turned and said, "You were right, teacher, when you spoke from Romans tonight. Many times we do not do what we know we should do, and again we do what we feel in our hearts is not right. We have no good, unchanging standards to follow. I want to believe in God and accept His standards you have been teaching us from the Bible." No, the image was not effaced. Indeed, on the whole, I have found it easier to deal with these young minds who glibly deny all God-consciousness and moral-consciousness, than with those who for five, six, or seven decades responded to this inner testimony but perverted it by worshiping idols for gods.

Due to the operation of God's common grace, however, man's work of suppressing the truth is in turn counteracted by God. Common grace is God's attitude of favor toward men as men, not toward them specifically as saved or unsaved. It has a twofold work. In part, it is God's grace in restraining the heathen from realizing their full potential for evil. It is thus a restraining influence of God holding sinful men back from being as wicked as they are capable of being. But it also has another function. It is God's common grace that "maketh his sun to rise on the evil and on the good, and sendeth rain on the just and the unjust" (Matt. 5:45). He thus gives men the opportunity to realize that God is good and longsuffering to sinful men. He sends His good gifts to them, that they might turn to Him, but they will not. Common grace also enables them to do acts of civil righteousness, such as to love their families and nations. Their reaction, however, due to the nature of unbelief, is always to suppress the truth of this witness of God to them. Therefore, they are without excuse! The heathen are not yearning for God and for His Christ, but are rather resisting the witness of general revelation and common grace.

We do, however, have a point of contact in our witness to them. They are still men, in the image of God, in these important, unchanging aspects. No matter how low they may fall into animal-like behavior they are still men—still conscious, at least to some small extent, of their need and with some yearning to rise above their plight. If they were not men in the image of God we could not communicate with them. The very presupposition of missions is that they have a God-consciousness, and so we can speak to them of God. We do not begin our witness to them in a void, but with the knowledge God has already spoken to them and is speaking to them.

It is not that we can simply build on their sense of God and bring them to God merely by giving them more information! No. It will only be rejected unless our witness is accompanied by the sovereign act of God's Holy Spirit in regenerating them. Not common grace, but special, supernatural grace is needed to bring men into His kingdom.

Since we have a point of contact, or perhaps a point of attack, we can talk to them. We can witness, and we can reason. We can tell them of the God of creation and providence and know that these are not meaningless concepts to them. We can go on to show them the traditional arguments for the existence of God, that the God we postulate from the Bible exists, and know that this will strike a responsive chord in their hearts even if they proceed to suppress it.

This method of witness is useful to teach them more of God, man, the universe, and their true relationship, and to drive the one opposing the truth further into the corner of illogic and contradiction. But we must remember that the door to the kingdom of God is not opened by the power and persuasion of human reasoning alone, nor by any other human effort. Forced admissions leave the mind of the same opinion still. Nominal head assent is still heart rejection. The kicking against the pricks of the reasoning, which is goading them into a corner, soon begins again in some other direction. Why? Because men are not argued into the kingdom of God; they are born into it.

Such reasoning is of great value when done in a spirit of love for the unbeliever. If he has set his mind and ideas on a throne of rebellion against God, he must be humbled by having those ideas defeated if he is to yield to God. The yielding will not follow without the gracious work of the Holy Spirit, however, which we must pray for as we witness. Paul effectively used a reasoning approach in his Athens sermon, which we will deal with on another occasion. But Paul in 1 Corinthians 1 shows the presuppositions behind his preaching in verses 22-24. "For the Jews require a sign, and the Greeks seek after wisdom. But we preach Christ crucified, unto the Jews a stumblingblock, and unto the Greeks foolishness; but unto them which are called, both Jews and Greeks, Christ the power of God, and the wisdom of God." The Greeks wanted wisdom, and Paul was willing to reason with them, but it is only Christ who is the power of God who changes men's lives. This brings us then to the other basic presupposition of missions that we must consider—that of the power of Christ to save through His gospel.

The Power of Christ to Save

In 1 Corinthians 1:24 we see this presupposition in Paul's preaching: that the gospel of Christ was completely adequate to save sinful men and would save all whom God would call. He had witnessed that power in operation from the beginning of His preaching. When Paul and Barnabas turned to preach to the Gentiles, we read, "For so hath the Lord commanded us, saying, I have set thee to be a light of the Gentiles, that thou shouldest be for salvation unto the ends of the earth. And when the Gentiles heard this, they were glad, and glorified the word of the Lord: and as many as were ordained to eternal life believed" (Acts 13:47-48). God had His own elect, chosen before the foundation of the world, and when Paul preached the gospel to them, God called them into faith.

This must be the hope and expectation of every missionary preacher. With men dead in trespasses and sins and in rebellion against God's truth, preaching would be futile if it were not for the power of God's calling, the supernatural internal call that God gives in His own time to His elect when the external call of the gospel goes out. In Ephesians 1, Paul is talking about the subject of election, predestination, and calling. In verse 19, he prays that they might know the hope of God's calling and "the exceeding greatness of his power toward us, who believe according to the working of his mighty power." It is according to the working of His mighty power that called ones believe. Without the operation of the Holy Spirit in regeneration, none could enter the kingdom.

The presupposition of God's election is behind our preaching to spiritually dead men. The doctrine of election, if properly understood, is not a handicap to evangelistic zeal, but rather its stimulus. We preach because we know it is not hopeless. God's elect must hear, and He will save them. The elect are many and exist in all places. Their salvation awaits our coming with the gospel, and it is our responsibility to reach them with it.

The doctrine of election ought not to be preached to Christians only to comfort and reassure them. When it is presented, it should be followed with an equal emphasis on the Christian's responsibility that springs from his election. We are elected and saved to serve (Eph. 2:8-10). Paul, after emphasizing to these Ephesian Christians the matter of their salvation by God's sovereign grace in 2:8-9, immediately reminds them of this in verse 10. "For we are his workmanship, created in Christ Jesus unto good works, which God hath before ordained that we should walk in them." The doctrine of election should be a stimulus to good works and especially to witnessing.

The power of Christ working through His gospel is adequate to save any man of any nation. Paul is saying this in Romans 1:16: "For I am not ashamed of the gospel of Christ: for it is the power of God unto salvation to every one that believeth; to the Jew first, and also to the Greek."

Negatively stated, it is neither education nor modern science that can transform men's lives from sinners to saints—nor is it western civilization and culture. These not infrequently have a worse effect, increasing crime and juvenile delinquency in heathen lands. The principles of democratic government and the moral and legal codes of western democracies cannot deliver men from spiritual darkness either.

Putting it positively, there is only salvation in the name of Christ and the gospel that bears His name. Only He can break the bondage of sin. It is the faithful preaching of His Word that is needed on the mission field today. The power is in the gospel as the Holy Spirit uses it. It does not need to be accompanied by any show of miracles or unintelligible babble of tongues.

A few years ago in Japan, a small group of discouraged missionaries leaving their work, and some their missions, were going to the mountains to pray for some manifestation of supernatural power to make them more effective preachers. Others followed until about 35 were gathered. They did no preaching, only continued in prayer and waiting. The weeks passed into months and the months to years without witnessing. Wasted opportunities! Finally, after two years, they dwindled down, some taking up secular work teaching English in colleges and others returning to the United States. They gave up, defeated! Some turned to spiritual pride. One claimed he was so advanced he did not need to read the Bible any more. They made shipwrecks of their missionary ministries because they did not trust the adequacy of the power of the gospel, nor the way the Lord was using it! We must preach the gospel and leave the results to Him—that is His responsibility. If the heathen will not hear the gospel, they will not believe, though one went back to them from the dead, our Lord declared. It is not miracles, but faithful preaching of the gospel—the power of God—that is needed. Then the invisible miracle of regeneration will take place and visible fruit will follow. Let us understand the basis and presuppositions of missions that we may not be deceived by unlearned men, nor discouraged by difficulties and slow growth. Men's hearts are hard, but God's Word is powerful and "in due season we shall reap if we faint not."

Questions for Study and Discussion

1. What are the two basic presuppositions with which we must face missionary work?
2. What did man lose in the fall? What is man's present spiritual condition?
3. What aspects of the image of God in man were not lost in the fall?
4. What is the true nature of unbelief?
5. What is God's common grace? What is its twofold work? How does it help the missionary in his witness?
6. How effective was the power of Christ to save the sinner in St. Paul's opinion? (Give scriptural evidence.)
7. Why is the doctrine of election a stimulus to missionary work?
8. How is the power of God principally manifested in missionary work?

3

"To where did Christ direct that His gospel be taken? 'To all nations.' So accustomed are we to hearing this, that the extraordinary nature of it is perhaps missed by us."

The Commission of Missions

O ur Lord's greatest concern on His last day on earth before His ascension, according to the presentation of the writers of the Gospels, was for the worldwide proclamation of His gospel. Matthew, Mark, and Luke in Acts each recount the event and give Christ's commission to preach His gospel to all the world. Matthew gives the greatest detail. Let us then examine the Great Commission as recorded by Matthew 28:18-20. "And Jesus came and spake unto them, saying, All power is given unto me in heaven and in earth. Go ye therefore, and teach all nations, baptizing them in the name of the Father, and of the Son, and of the Holy Ghost: Teaching them to observe all things whatsoever I have commanded you: and, lo, I am with you always, even unto the end of the world. Amen."

Who Should Go?

First, let us consider by *whom* it was given, and *to whom*. The commission to preach the gospel is Christ's commission. It is here specifically based on the universal authority given Him by the Father. With His authority, the apostles were sent out to be the first missionaries. "As my Father hath sent me, even so send I you," He said to them (John 20:21). They were to go with His continuous presence: "Lo I am with you always" (Matt. 28:20). As He had said earlier, "When he putteth forth his sheep, he goeth before them" (John 10:4). It would have been folly to go without that presence.

He was standing there on the Mount, however. How would He be present everywhere? Matthew does not tell us, but closes with this divine promise. Luke in Acts 1, however, gives us the story. He ascended from that place on the mountain in order to be everywhere, to assure His omnipresence. In His ascension He laid aside the limitations of earthly life and resumed the glory and omnipresence of His heavenly one, with all authority in heaven and earth.

The commission was from Christ, and it was to the apostles. This is, I believe, the primary significance here. The commission was given directly to the apostles and not to disciples as Christians in general. Matthew mentions specifically that it was to the eleven (Matt. 28:16), and Luke says that it was to "the apostles whom he had chosen" (Acts 1:2) who had assembled on His orders to meet Him. It is, of course, perfectly true that every Christian is and must be a witness, but that is not the immediate and primary significance here. Rather, here we see the Great Commission being given to the apostles as Christ's chosen office bearers.

Our Lord Jesus Christ had within Himself all the Old Testament offices of prophet, priest, and king. But various Scriptures make it clear that when He chose His apostles, He chose them to assume these offices and left them to administer His Church as His office bearers, His officers. As prophets they were to proclaim the Word of God; as priests, to dispense the mercy of God, and, as kings, to have the spiritual oversight or rule over the people of God through the discipline and government of the Church.

Man was created as a rational, religious, and responsible being, as we have observed, with self-consciousness, God-consciousness and moral-consciousness, with knowledge, righteousness, and holiness. To reach man and develop him in these three aspects of His nature during Old Testament times, God provided for him prophets, priests, and kings, and, when Christ came to make the supreme provision for men, He had within Himself the three God-given offices of prophet, priest, and king of His Church. The *Westminster Larger Catechism*, question 42, asks: "Why was our Mediator called Christ?" The answer is, "Our Mediator was called Christ, because he was anointed with the Holy Ghost above measure; and so set apart, and fully furnished with all authority and ability, to execute the office of prophet, priest and king of his Church, in the estate both of his humiliation and exaltation." The *Heidelberg Catechism*, question 31, asks: "Why is He called Christ, that is, Anointed?" The answer is:

> Because He is ordained of God the Father, and anointed with the Holy Spirit, to be our chief Prophet and Teacher, who has fully revealed to us the secret counsel and will of God concerning our redemption; and our only High Priest, who by the one sacrifice of His body has redeemed us, and makes continual intercession for us with the Father; and our eternal King, who governs us by His Word and Spirit, and defends and preserves us in the salvation obtained for us.

Christ received these three offices from His Father, and when He commissioned His apostles, He said, "As my Father hath sent me, even so send I you." He then breathed on the apostles saying, "Receive ye the Holy Ghost" and gave them His authority to administer and discipline His Church. John 20:21-23 reads: "Then said Jesus to them again, Peace be unto you: as my Father hath sent me, even so send I you. And when he had said this, he breathed on them, and saith unto them, Receive ye the Holy Ghost: whosoever sins ye remit, they are remitted unto them; and whosoever sins ye retain, they are retained." The apostles thus had these three offices of the Church invested in them, and for a time they were the sole officers of the Church.

But the apostles are no longer here to be the officers of the Church and to execute this Great Commission they received from their Lord. Who has taken their place and received the offices? The Episcopalians claim their bishops to be the true successors of the apostles and to be able to pass the succession on by laying on of hands. This, we believe, is to be rejected as having no biblical foundation and assuming a too mechanical view of the succession. The Bible does give us the answer, however, as we see there the development of the permanent offices of the Church corresponding to these three special offices of prophet, priest, and king. These permanent offices are those of the preaching elder or minister, administering the Word of God (1 Tim. 5:17); deacons, administering the mercy of God (Acts 6:2-6); and elders, administering the spiritual rule of God in His Church (Acts 14:23; 20:17, 28).

Christ's Great Commission then was given to His apostles and passed on from them to the subsequent officers of His Church. It is certainly the responsibility of the officers of Christ's Church today, then, to carry out this missionary commission of taking the gospel to all the nations. God will surely hold them responsible to discharge this responsibility.

How Should They Be Sent?

But how should they discharge it? For one thing, they should stimulate interest in this great task, encouraging every Christian to help to take Christ's gospel to the nations, seeking to stir up and move every Christian to be a sender. Every Christian should be an active witness. Peter made that clear in 1 Peter 3:15 when he wrote; "Be ready always to give an answer to every man that asketh you a reason of the hope that is in you with meekness and fear." Every believer has within him the general offices, even as the Church officers have the special offices, the offices of prophet, priest and king. Peter has already reminded them of that in 1 Peter 2:9, "Ye are a chosen generation, a royal [kingly] priesthood, an holy nation, a peculiar people; that ye should bring forth the praises of him who hath called you out of darkness into his marvelous light."

Here then participation in fulfilling the Great Commission comes down to every believer, from Christ through His church officers. Every believer must discharge his general offices for Christ; (1) by witnessing the Word as far as he can, wherever he is; (2) by praying and giving in mercy for the relief of the needy and the proclamation of the Word to all nations; and (3) by ruling himself according to God's Word as a testimony to the unconverted of the Lord's grace.

When a person volunteers to go, the church officers should examine him and, if satisfied of his preparation and ability, do all they can to help him be sent. For "How can they [the heathen in the nations of the world] hear without a preacher? And how can they preach except they be sent?" (Rom. 10:14-15). When this system is not followed and church officers fail to discharge their responsibilities, great difficulty is placed in the way of the volunteer. Or if volunteers ignore the church and go out alone, then they lack the supervision they need, and often incompetence and wasted efforts ensue.

The church officers must stir and challenge the believers to be senders and to participate themselves in enabling the nations to hear the gospel by giving to the support of others who will thus be their representatives. The officers must also seek to raise interest in volunteers going. How will they do this? Our Lord put the emphasis first on prayer. "Pray ye the Lord of the harvest, that he will send forth laborers into his harvest" (Matt. 9:38). The session should pray, the minister should pray publicly, and all should pray at home for volunteers and greater giving for missions.

But teaching is also important—teaching from the pulpit, in the Sunday school, and in various church organizations. The teaching should start with the basis of missions, behind the command to send out the gospel to the *reason* for the command in the plan of God for this age—the expansion of His dominion to some in all nations before His kingdom comes in its fulfillment. When these things are constantly held before His Church, giving will increase. There will follow also the next step in the advancement of the missionary enterprise through the local church.

God the Holy Spirit will lay the burden upon some heart to volunteer to go to the mission field. How will that call come? It is hard to say. The testimony of different missionaries indicates a great diversity of ways in which God has led. Some have said the call is the command to go, which reveals Christ's vital concern to get the gospel to every nation. Assuredly, it will come in conjunction with the Word of God and probably through the ministry of the Word through the Church. A burden to participate in the fulfillment of the command to take the gospel to the nations by actually going will grow into a deep conviction that this is the will of God and that this burden is from God. If it is from God, it must be motivated by the love of God and aim at His glory by seeking to bring the lost into His kingdom. The motive of compassion for the lost state of the heathen will be there, but the important thing is that it must be based on the love of God, loving a world of lost sinners loved by God.

It is not likely that the impulse to be a missionary will come from a dream, a vision, or an audible voice in the night. The voice calling Paul into Macedonia was not his call to be a missionary. But the burden to serve the Lord anywhere He wills, and in particular to carry the gospel to the nations, will be the possession of those called, based on the commands of Christ and the needs of men, motivated by God's love and aimed at His glory. As to the place of future missionary effort, one may feel that the Lord wants him in a particular land, but more often this is a conviction that comes only after counseling with others who have experience and knowledge of the needs of fields. The Lord uses such human instruments in guiding a candidate, as the experience of many veteran missionaries attests.

The third step, as the Church through its officers seeks to discharge its missionary responsibility to the Great Commission, is the designating, ordaining, and commissioning of the missionary. That this is the work of the Church through its officers appears in Acts 13:1-4. Here Paul and Barnabas were sent out. The Antioch church was founded by Christians from Jerusalem witnessing there; then Barnabas was sent by the Jerusalem church to preach for them. He sent for Paul in Tarsus. Together they labored for one year, and many were added to the Church. Next, the Holy Spirit spoke to the leaders of this church and said, "Send Paul and Barnabas out on the mission I have set for them." So they prayed and laid their hands on them and sent them forth.

They were sent out by Christ through the officers of His instituted Church and went forth to convert the heathen and establish churches. They clearly continued to feel their responsibility to the home church, for after a time they returned there to report (14:27). They then continued under the direction of the church, which sent them next to Jerusalem to resolve the new missionary problem of whether the converted Gentiles should be circumcised. It was the church as instituted, as organized with officers—not just as a group of individual Christians—that sent them out and that assembled in Jerusalem to decide the missionary problem. It was the church council that sent out its decision to all the churches.

How Many Should Go?

This then raises the question of the governing and sending out of missionaries today. Should they go out by themselves? Are they to be sent out by local congregations directly? Should they be sent out by local congregations working together with others of that denomination, working through one denominational board? Or are they to be sent out by church officers working through independent missionary agencies?

As to the first, going out alone is not the biblical example. It has grave defects and limitations. Missionaries need the counsel of fellow ministers and their overall supervision even more on a foreign field than at home. Working alone tends to lead to unorganized and inefficient labor. The biblical example is the local church officers, as those governing the local church and responsible for discharging the missionary commission, sending out the missionaries with the authority of Christ. The other two questions following this are secondary. Many local congregations want to participate in forwarding the missionary work before they can assume the full support of a missionary. What is more natural than that they should work with others of like faith to do together what they cannot do alone?

If they send their support to their denominational mission board, then they should be sure that their responsibility does not end there. The church through its officers must maintain an active interest in that work and be sure that those to whom they have delegated the supervision of their missionary effort are doing it according to the directions agreed to by the whole denomination, which set up the board. The methods of operation of the missionaries on the fields should be well defined so all churches have a clear understanding of what is being or should be done.

If the support goes to an independent agency, then at least it should be to one of similar beliefs, comprised of board members who are experienced officers in the church, preferably of their own denomination. That way, they will be assured that those to whom they are delegating the supervision of their missionary effort are capable and responsible supervisors.

It is interesting to note that some Reformed churches in Holland maintain no foreign board, but that local churches support their own missionaries directly, with their Synod appointing a committee to supervise the missionaries! It at least saves the expense of home board overhead, although if there were very many missionaries it would certainly seem to be difficult for a committee of busy ministers to do it full justice. The Christian Reformed Church in America has a foreign board, but each missionary must receive a call from a local church to be its missionary whereupon he becomes a regular member of their consistory or session. This system has the advantage of drawing the church and missionary close together.

To summarize our conclusion thus far, the local church officers are indeed the heirs of the apostles' special offices of prophet, priest, and king: preaching, serving, and ruling for Christ, who gave the apostles, and through them the church's officers today, His Great Commission.

Where Should the Gospel Be Taken?

To where did Christ direct that His gospel be taken? "To all nations."
So accustomed are we to hearing this, that the extraordinary nature of it is
perhaps missed by us. It was not a commission to a Roman emperor, or to the
commander of his armies. Even they had not conquered all nations! Nor was it
a commission to learned men trained in international matters and the world's
learning. Rather, it was given to Galilean fishermen and tax collectors, simple
folk with little education and worldly experience. Extraordinary indeed! No
wonder Paul was to write in 1 Corinthians 1:26-27, "For ye see your calling,
brethren, how that not many wise men after the flesh, not many mighty, not
many noble, are called, but God hath chosen the foolish things of the world
to confound the wise; and God hath chosen the weak things of the world to
confound the things which are mighty."

How could it possibly work? Because the commissioner was God! The
work was His work; His power and authority were behind it! It was His plan
for this age, a plan which goes back before the foundation of the world, that in
His final kingdom some from all peoples of the world should be represented,
symbols of His Victory over the enemy of souls and His complete conquest by
love and salvation.

Nearly 20 centuries later, how well are we doing at fulfilling this commission to all nations? Is it not strange that today over 90 percent of the world's
ministers are ministering to those already established in churches; those who
hear the Word two or three times a week—while less than five percent strive to
take the gospel to those nations and tongues where it is little known or quite
unknown? Is this fulfilling His commission? Surely the church of Christ today
needs to look again at its calling and commission! Surely it needs to hear again
its Lord's command, "Go to all the nations."

What Are the Servants to Do?

Finally, what did He commission His servants to do? His instructions
seem to unfold in three simple parts, or at least one theme with two divisions.
The imperative to make disciples is followed by two participles: baptizing and
teaching.

To make disciples is the first and main theme. Preach for the conversion
of the heathen! This is the first and immediate step of missions—present the

claims of Christ the King to a sinful and rebellious people. Call to repentance for sin and a yielding to Christ for the forgiveness of sins. Preach the gospel of salvation that the lost might hear, believe, and be saved. This is the missionary's task.

Then these disciples are to be baptized in the Triune name of God. The name which reveals the way of our salvation: the Father who sent the Son, the Son who purchased our redemption, and the Holy Spirit who regenerates us and applies the finished work of Christ to those whose eyes He has opened to believe.

The sacrament of baptism is for the officers of the church to administer. At first the missionary can do it, but he cannot be there forever. His task must be to help organize the believers into a church with officers, as Paul did. Then, that they can do the work of a church, that is, they can (1) insure the preaching of the Word, to themselves and to the neighborhood; (2) maintain the true administration of the sacraments; and (3) maintain the proper administration of discipline. The establishment of the indigenous, local church is inherent in this second instruction of the commission.

But there is a third injunction, or second part of the main theme to make disciples: "Teaching them to observe all his commandments." Indoctrination. That is what it means. If one is to indoctrinate, he must first be trained himself. There is a body of truth, a body of doctrine, to be taught. It is derived from the Scriptures. It is not enough just to know some of the fundamentals of the faith and not to be aware of the full system of the faith summarized in one of the great Reformed confessions like the *Belgic* or *Westminster Confession*. The difference is something like that of confronting planks lying in a row on the ground and those planks fitted together into the framework of a house. We need to know the system of construction and be teachers of it.

We need to train others to preach it also if the Commission is to be carried on. Paul urged Timothy in 2 Timothy 2:1-2, 15, "Thou therefore, my son, be strong in the grace that is in Christ Jesus. And the things that thou hast heard of me among many witnesses, the same commit thou to faithful men, who shall be able to teach others also . . . study to shew thyself approved unto God, a workman that needeth not to be ashamed, rightly dividing [discerning] the word of truth." The establishing of theological schools for the training of ministers of the gospel on the field is part of this teaching when the churches are ready for it. The commission is ours, officers of Christ's Church, heirs of the apostles. The task of forwarding it belongs to every Christian! Let us not fail! Let us say with Paul in 2 Timothy 2:10, "Therefore I endure all things for the elect's sakes, that they may also obtain the salvation which is in Christ Jesus with eternal glory." Amen.

Questions for Study and Discussion

1. By whom was the Great Commission given, and where is it recorded?
2. To whom did Christ directly give the Great Commission?
3. Why are church officers today responsible for carrying out the Great Commission? How should they carry out this responsibility?
4. How must every believer discharge his responsibility in fulfilling the general offices of Christ?
5. What are some of the factors in a call to be a missionary?
6. Who is responsible for ordaining and commissioning the missionary? Where is this described in Scripture?
7. Which is more scriptural: a missionary going out independent of any church organization, or one sent by the officers of the local church through a mission board? Give reasons for your answer.
8. What percentage of the world's ministers are taking the gospel to areas where Christ has never been named or where very little is known of His grace?
9. What types of people were first called to be foreign missionaries?
10. Outline the content and meaning of the Great Commission.

Part 2:
The Confrontation

4

Communication and Missions

When the missionary goes to the foreign land, his immediate objective is to present the gospel of Christ so that the people will understand his message. As he presents the message, he must diligently pray that they will believe and be saved. He applies himself to learning the language and to discovering all he can about the native religions and culture. As he begins his witnessing, however, he is immediately faced with a serious problem. The Christian religion and terminology are either unknown to them, or so little known as to be completely misinterpreted by them. Their minds have been so long steeped in their own religious concepts and vocabulary, that even when he uses terminology for such basic ideas as God, sin, holiness, repentance, and salvation, they are interpreting these terms in the context of their own religious usage and thus making quite different concepts of them. Thus, when the missionary speaks of God or sin, even when he uses their language for these terms, the words are heard by them not with his meaning but with theirs. How shall the missionary communicate his message so that the pagan mind can understand it? Let us consider the problem first, and then the answer to it.

The Problem

The problem is occasioned by the prior concepts of the pagan mind. What, however, is our responsibility as we witness to them? We know it is not to bring regeneration. That is not our responsibility. It is not within our power. Regeneration is the work of God and rests solely within His sovereignty. What is it then? In Romans 10:13-15, 17, we have it laid out before us. The chronological order, if the heathen are to call upon the Lord and be saved, tracing it backwards in verse 14, is, first, they must hear; then believe; then call on the Lord.

"How then shall they call on him in whom they have not believed? And how shall they believe in him of whom they have not heard? And how shall they hear without a preacher?" This is repeated in verse 17: "So then faith cometh by hearing, and hearing by the word of God." Of the three—hearing, believing, and calling on the Lord—we cannot cause the latter two. We can only cause them to hear audibly. This is the immediate goal of the preacher: to bring the gospel message within the sound of their ears.

Is this the hearing referred to in verse 17? The Bible speaks of two kinds of hearing, or possibly three. "Hearing they hear not, neither do they understand" (Matt. 13:13). Does it mean, "Hearing, they comprehend not nor understand spiritually?" Those who "hear not," then, hear with neither natural comprehension nor spiritual understanding. They hear the words but do not understand them. It is likely, however, that verse 17 refers to the last type of hearing mentioned above, the hearing of spiritual understanding, evangelical obedience. But in any case the sequence must be (1) *hearing* the audible words of the Word of God; (2) *understanding* them with some comprehension; (3) then, with the eyes of the understanding (the heart) being opened by the regeneration of the Holy Spirit, *believing* what is heard, spiritual understanding.

In this sequence, surely the responsibility of the missionary preacher is not only to cause the heathen to hear the Word of God audibly but also with some comprehension. Surely it is his responsibility to study the religion, the customs, the usage, and the concepts of the religious vocabulary he uses. Then, he will know how to present his message so they will know what he is talking about. This "hearing," at least, is his responsibility. The "hearing" of faith must be the gift of God. We are not called upon to give just a superficial presentation, but our task is to bring as much understanding of our message as is possible. It may take some time. When it is understood, it will be followed by either rejection or faith.

This *natural comprehension* will mean only that the claims of the gospel have been sufficiently made clear so that the hearers know that to believe involves a confession of sin before a holy God, a renunciation of self and sin, and a yielding to the supreme and sole lordship of Jesus Christ. This requires making clear the antithesis between identification with Christ and continuation with the world. This kind of natural comprehension can only be followed by rejection of the gospel by the natural man. Rejection, that is, unless the Holy Spirit moves with regenerating power to open the eyes of discernment from an inadequate natural comprehension to spiritual understanding and faith. It is the initial task of the missionary to bring the first hearing, the audible hearing of the gospel, seeking to bring a maximum of comprehension. Only the power of the Holy Spirit can change this into the latter hearing—the hearing of faith.

One reason for *easy believism*, the quick, easy response of claimed belief later repudiated, is that people do not understand the message but are interpreting it according to their own pagan concepts. What they believe is not the gospel but their own idea of it. They later fall away when they learn the truth about it.

The task is not as formidable, however, as it may at first seem to be. The reason lies not with men but with God. He has prepared the way for their hearing with some understanding. We have previously referred to the fact that He has created man in His own image and left within fallen man the seed of religion (*semen religiones*), particularly the imprint on the human heart of God-consciousness. Further, He has revealed Himself in the rest of creation, for "the heavens declare the glory of God and the firmament showeth his handiwork" (Ps. 19:1). Still further, He has not left Himself without a witness of His common graciousness to all men in that He sends them rain and sunshine, and, although He has given some of them up to practice the great moral debauchery they desired, His Spirit still strives with them to restrain them from falling into the full evil potential of which they are otherwise capable. It is our God who has been thus speaking to the heathen down through the centuries, preserving them as His rational, moral, and religious creatures, and thus preserving a point of contact so that the missionary can communicate the heavenly message to their earthly senses.

The argument of Paul in Romans 10 is in striking support of the fact that God has always been speaking to the pagan Gentile world. "So then faith cometh by hearing, and hearing by the word of God. But I say, have they not heard? Yes verily, their sound went into all the earth, and their words unto the ends of the world" (Rom. 10:17-18). Paul here wants to show that God's present offering of His gospel to the Gentiles, through Paul's preaching, is not an absolutely new interest of God's in the Gentiles but just a fulfilling of it. To do this, in verse 18, he quotes from Psalm 19:4, and says the "sound" and "words" of God went out to all the world! When did this take place? When did, or when do, the heathen hear the Word of God, the speech of God?

Regarding this verse, John Calvin, in his commentary on Romans, says that the heavens and the earth

> have a sort of tongue of their own to declare the perfections of God . . . .
> God has already from the beginning manifested His divinity to the Gentiles,
> though not by the preaching of men, yet by the testimony of His creatures; for
> though the gospel was then silent among them, yet the whole workmanship
> of heaven and earth did speak and make known its author by its preaching. It
> hence appears, that the Lord . . . did not yet (heretofore) so withdraw from the
> Gentiles the knowledge of Himself, but that He even kept alive some sparks
> of it among them . . . He showed by this prelude that He designed to make
> Himself known at length to them also.

Our God not only has never withdrawn His witness to the heathen, but also, by this very fact, has shown His intention someday of revealing Himself to them with far more clarity, says Calvin. When we go to them with the gospel, we can rejoice to know that day has arrived for them, that God has sent us to them, and that He has His elect among them. Because He has maintained His testimony without them in nature and within them, we are able to communicate His message to them.

But what have the heathen done with the truth God has been witnessing to them? In Romans 1:18, Paul makes this clear. They have suppressed it, held it down, distorted and perverted it (v. 21), and worshiped and served the creature more than the Creator (v. 25). This is the basis for the great barrier as we seek to get them to understand the gospel. Just as barnacles can cluster on an oyster until the original creature is almost unrecognizable, so men have so suppressed the sense of God within them—by substituting false deities and perverting the religious and moral ideas to which their consciences testify—that the original is scarcely recognizable. In Japan, the word for God, *Kami,* has only a polytheistic significance. Sin, *taumi*, means crime, or actually, only being caught in it, and is held by a Shinto sect to be like dust on the hands, which can be washed off. Purity has to do only with avoiding ceremonial defilement; and salvation is deliverance from the Buddhist idea of unending reincarnations. In our next discussion, we will go into such things further. Suffice it to say here that behind these perverted concepts lies a conscience much closer to the truth. The barnacle barriers to understanding what the Christian means by such terms can be knocked away, by those who understand their origin and structure, and who carefully labor at it. The heathen are still in the image of God. God has been speaking to them through the ages. This is our hope of successfully communicating to them as we witness. *Easy believism* is based on a false understanding, and is followed by a dropping out of the church. There is a big turnover among Japan's churches because of belief based on an unreal hearing! When they do understand what is being taught, there is one of two reactions: either they reject it or they delight in it and seek to learn more.

Presenting the Gospel

But now let us go on to consider the presentation. What should be our presentation as we strive to communicate God's message of redemption to the lost? We must approach them as those with whom God has already been dealing, but those who have terribly distorted and misrepresented His revelation. We must strive to be used as messengers of God's Son and His Word to them. Is this not the way Paul approached the heathen Gentiles?

Let us look at his confrontation with the heathen at Lystra after he had worked a miracle and they interpreted it to mean that their gods, Jupiter and Mercurius, had returned to them. "We . . . preach unto you that ye should turn from these vanities unto the living God, which made heaven, and earth, and the sea, and all things that are therein: Who in times past suffered all nations to walk in their own ways. Nevertheless he left not himself without witness, in that he did good, and gave us rain from heaven, and fruitful seasons, filling our hearts with food and gladness," (Acts 14:15-17). In verse 15, he points out that their worship is in vain and should be rejected. He also says that the missionaries have come to tell them of the Creator, "the living God" who made all things. In verses 16-17, he states that although God has thus far suffered their rebellious ways, He has been witnessing to them through His good blessings bestowed through nature. Now God wants them to turn to Him in truth. This is His theme, stated in verse 15: although they had been rejecting Him, He was still seeking them.

Paul clearly rejected, and called on them to reject, their erroneous concepts of God. Equally clearly, he told them that it was the God of the skies over their heads and the earth they stood upon who had never ceased to witness to them nor be good to them, not some foreign god (even though they had tried to make Him a foreigner by banishing Him from their minds). He had come to tell them about the only true, living, Creator God.

In his recorded sermon to the Athenian intellectuals, Paul used the same approach (Acts 17:16ff). Verse 16 tells us that Paul was greatly agitated by the sight of Athen's idolatry. The symbols of their polytheistic beliefs were everywhere. He, therefore, did not limit his preaching to the synagogues, where the Jews would hear him, but went out into the marketplace and preached Jesus Christ and His resurrection from the dead. It was a new message for Athens and, apparently, was presented in such a way that it raised the curiosity of the sophisticated city men. They arranged to have him speak before the Council of the Areopagus, the most venerable Athenian court, which met at that time in the Agora. It had great respect because of its ancient origin. Even under the Romans, the council had supreme authority in religious matters and the power to appoint public lecturers, even exercising some control over them in the interests of maintaining public order.

How should Paul begin before this illustrious and learned gathering? He began as he did in Lystra, by introducing them to the God who was not foreign to the land but who was the sovereign over it, "the Lord of heaven and earth," even though they acknowledged that they did not know Him. Paul cleverly started by referring to the altar addressed "To the Unknown God" as evidence that their ignorance was not of His existence. Paul knew that there was an awareness stamped on their hearts as God's image bearers, but that there was an ignorance of the truth about Him. Their worship was thus in ignorance and error. Paul had come to tell them the truth about Him.

Paul went on to point out that the true God is God of all the universe, of Athens also then, and, therefore, He, the maker of the earth, could not be tied down to any Athenian temple made with men's hands! What would He do with temple food offerings, He who was the Giver of life to all things that grow? As to the people of Lystra, he also called their attention to God's common grace in giving them all that they possessed, and he said that God had done all this for them that they might seek Him as their Lord. The heathen almost always have special stories attributing divine origin to themselves. The Athenians prided themselves that they were not immigrants but that they had sprung from the soil of their native Attica, and were far superior to non-Greeks, whom they called barbarians. But Paul with one thrust undercuts this idea of racial superiority and at the same time drives home again the fact that the true God is the God of all men, the one universal God. "He hath made of one blood all nations of men," he declares (Acts 17:26). The unity of the human race as descended from the one man Adam is fundamental to the salvation of men through the one Savior, the God-man, Jesus Christ.

Paul then again impresses them with the fact that he is not introducing a foreign God who lives far away, but One who has always been near to them. To make this important point even more striking, he uses language from one of their own writers (Acts 17:28). The words used are from an address to Zeus by his son Minos, one which must have been well-known to Paul because we see him quoting from it again in Titus 1:12. It runs,

> They fashioned a tomb for thee, O holy and high one—
> The Cretans, always liars, evil beasts, idle bellies!
> But thou art not dead: thou livest and abidest forever,
> For in thee we live and move and have our being.
>
> —Epimenides, Cretica

And then he makes a direct quote from another source, one of their poets, "For we are also his offspring."

From these things that they acknowledge they know about God, which they must have derived from God's witness to Himself in general revelation,

Paul wants to show them how they have suppressed and distorted the truth. They have made images of metal with which to worship God and thus have worshiped the creature more than the Creator! This shows great ignorance, but God is willing to overlook it now if they will repent of it as a great sin against God, and turn from idols to serve the living and true God. There is no other way to escape the judgment of God, who is going to judge the whole world by One whom He has appointed. This One He has proved to be entirely adequate for this solemn task, for God raised Him from the dead.

Such was the gist of Paul's sermon and his manner of presentation to these pagan, intellectual Greeks. He knew of their inner knowledge of God, stemming from their creation in God's image and God's revelation of Himself in nature. He even quoted from their religious altars and writers to prove that they acknowledged some smattering of this knowledge. But he immediately went on to show how they had suppressed and distorted it in creature worship. He warned them of God's wrath and judgment if they did not repent of this and told of God's mercy to overlook it if they would repent. Then he introduced the Judge whom God had provided and had demonstrated to be One of His own appointment by raising Him from the dead.

That was as far as he got. To sophisticated men, many of whom had no place for even the immortality of the soul, the idea of the resurrection of a dead body was beyond belief.

Many a missionary has found an almost identical reaction when he reached this great truth. Belief in the mighty works of the true God is unacceptable to the natural man until the mighty work of the Holy Spirit intervenes and regeneration takes place. Paul, no doubt, had they allowed him, would have gone on to present the saving work of the true God whom he was introducing to them, whose salvation was through the Judge who was also the Savior. It was because of this Savior's work that God would overlook their past idolatry if they repented and believed on Him.

The Reaction

What was the result of this kind of gentlemanly, but completely forthright, presentation of the Christian message? There were at first two different reactions. There usually are if the missionary has done his work well. And Paul had done his work well. His task was to make the message just as intelligible to his heathen audience as he could. He wanted them to hear it with as full a hearing as it was possible for the natural man to attain. He had done all he could to make the unknown known in terms they could understand. We may be sure his heart was full of prayer that God would bless the effort with the work of the Spirit in bringing regeneration and spiritual understanding.

The two reactions were these: Some mocked his presentation of the Christian message; Others felt an inner voice telling them that this was deserving of the most careful consideration. It was too close to their real, inner God-consciousness to resist so easily. They needed to hear more, and they said so. From those who went with him, some came to enlightenment and faith in Jesus Christ. These results are still the results a missionary today can expect if he makes the message clear to the unsaved. If he has not made its distinctiveness clear and has left vagueness in the people's minds so that they think of it merely as generally a good thing and similar to the best ideas in their own religions, he may get a ready response of acceptance from many when he gives an invitation to accept His Lord. But as time goes on, and they receive further instruction and enlightenment, and discover the exclusiveness and real meaning of the Christian message, they may well say, "This is not what I thought it was! I don't want this!" Then they will leave the church, causing much grief and damage to its testimony. The easy believism was based on a false belief.

But if the message has been made clear so that they have a real hearing of it—with a comprehension of its significance, of its exclusiveness, of its distinction from their pagan religious ideas, and of its real truth—then a desire to continue to learn more will probably reflect an inner hunger that is finding satisfaction in the truth and the working of the Holy Spirit. From such enlightened followers it will be only a matter of time until the Spirit who has begun His work among them will complete it, and some will come to saving faith.

How great is our privilege to be ambassadors of the living God and to communicate His precious message! May it ever be our aim to make it clear and plain that men may truly hear it from us, and that God the Holy Spirit may use our presentation to bring life everlasting to the lost.

Questions for Study and Discussion

1. What is the immediate object of the missionary upon arrival in a foreign land?

2. What is usually the first problem in communication faced by missionaries?

3. What is the responsibility of the missionary in bringing the heathen to the place of regeneration?

4. Is it enough to say that the missionary is responsible to cause the heathen to hear the Word of God audibly?

5. How does God prepare a human heart to hear His Word?

6. What have the heathen done with the truth that God has been witnessing to them, both through nature and within their own nature?

7. How should we present the gospel to the heathen? Give a scriptural example.

8. What two reactions did Paul usually receive when He presented the gospel to the heathen, and that we may expect today?

9. Name some important elements in the presentation of the gospel that help afford the listeners a real hearing of it.

5

Elenctics and Missions

"It behooves the missionary of God's special revelation to understand the pagan religion that he may be better able to expose to the non-Christian his own inner rebellion against the God who has not left Himself without a witness to him . . . ."

Why at is *elenctics*? A reference to the dictionary would indicate it to mean, "serving to refute." Its early Greek usage, as the verb *elengchein*, indicated a meaning of bringing to shame, and later to a conviction of guilt. It is this sense that we find in its New Testament usages. In Revelation 3:19 it appears as *rebuke*: "As many as I love; I rebuke and chasten." In John 16:8 it is translated *reprove*: "and when He [the Holy Spirit] is come, He will reprove the world of sin, and of righteousness, and of judgment."

As the word elenctics has been used in theology, it concerns the refutation of false religions. Specifically, then, in the light of the New Testament use of the word, to us elenctics is the refutation of a heathen religion in order to lead an individual to a conviction of his sin against God and to make a confession of Christ as his Savior. Such a refutation will of course entail a knowledge of the native religion, not only its surface manifestations but its basic principles, motives, and aims. The platform from which we undertake to bring conviction of sin to the heathen must always be a deep realization that we too have sought to suppress the truth of God, and that except for the grace of God would still be doing it. The basis of truly Christian elenctics must be God's special revelation in His Word and Son.

All religious activity of man, and therefore all religions, spring from the fact that when God created man in His image He made him, as we have already observed, a religious being, as well as rational and moral, with the seed of religion rooting in his ineradicable God-consciousness and moral-consciousness. Heathen religions spring from man's sinful suppression or restraining of this knowledge of God, and from the perversion of the revelation of God in nature. In taking up this subject of elenctics and missions then, we must consider what man has done with his God-consciousness and moral-consciousness in his religious expression. The field is vast, so for purposes of illustration we will choose the two ancient religions of Japan, where I have been working for the past dozen years: the religions of Shintoism and Buddhism.

Example: Shintoism

The question concerning God-consciousness is simply this: What have they done with God? We will begin with the Shintoists. The oldest written literature recording Shinto mythology is the *Kojiki*, written about 712 A.D. It opens with a reference to the time when the gods came into being, the first one being the god of the Center of Heaven, followed by two others. From these three all the others are derived.

Two important ones are Izanagi and Izanami, the former of whom makes the land of Japan and peoples it. It is thus a divine land with a divine people. They produced the Sun Goddess (Amaterasu Omikami) who sent her grandson to rule Japan, and thus also gave Japan a divine emperor. He arrived with three objects to symbolize his authority that are today national treasures and the symbol of authority of the emperor: the bronze mirror, sacred object of worship at the Ise Shrine of the Sun Goddess; the sword, sacred object of a Nagoya shrine; and the jewels, curved, jade beads, sacred object of the Imperial Palace shrine.

This grandson, Niniginomikoto, became the great grandfather of the first emperor, Jimmu, who started the line of divine emperors. It is interesting to note that although this event was supposed to have taken place in 660 B.C., neither bronze mirrors nor iron reached Japan until the Chinese immigration of the 4th century A.D., one thousand years later! The word *Shinto* means "The Way of the

Kami," *kami* being the native Japanese pronunciation for the Chinese ideograph *Shen*, the generic term for god or gods. In Shintoism, it has always had a plural significance unless referring to a particular deity. More than 100,000 shrines exist to worship the gods, usually in a grove of trees with the characteristic torii gate in front, while almost every home has its own little god shelf, the *kamidana*. The essence of Shintoism is ancestor worship.

The eight million gods of its pantheon of deities, or kami, vary in nature from the original mythological creator gods to the spirits of trees, mountains, fishing sites, foxes, crows, fertility objects, and the spirits of the deceased emperors, heroes, and ancestors. The greatest among these is the sun goddess, Amaterasu Omikami, the progenitor of the emperors, since she is held to have sent her grandson to found the Japanese imperial lineage. She is worshiped in the most venerated spot in Japan, the Grand Shrine of Ise. Today, once again, great efforts are being made by the government to circumvent the provisions of the new constitution for the separation of religion and state by restoring this shrine to national status and putting it on the government payroll. The worship of all these deities centers around the observance of ceremonies and festivals, which are intricately involved in home, community, and national life.

It is clear that the Shinto religion has ramifications for the Japanese that involve their total lives. Professor Ono, a Shinto scholar writing in *The Kami Way,* has declared, "Many parishioners are hardly aware of the extent to which they are linked to and unconsciously controlled by the shrine and all that it means" (p. 93). Again,

> The world of Shinto is not an isolated one. It is an all-inclusive one. It includes all things organic and inorganic. All nature, man, animals, mountains, rivers, herbs, and trees come into existence by virtue of the kami, and their limitless blessings contribute to the well-being of the world. The world is not in contrast with or in opposition to man. On the contrary, it is filled with the blessings of the kami and is developing through the power of harmony and cooperation. Shinto is not a pessimistic faith. It is an optimistic faith. This world is inherently good. That which interferes with man's happiness should be expelled. It belongs to another world. Man is a child of kami; he also is inherently good. Yet there is no clear line of distinction between himself and the kami. In one sense men are kami, and they will become kami. (p. 103)

A fascinating statement, is it not, in the light of what we have been considering thus far, that all men know that their blessings come from God, but then they suppress and distort this by giving credit and worship to the creature instead of their Creator? In this case they claim that their ancestors are the kami who have done all this for them!

What have the Shintoists done with God? Paul said that God "had left not himself without a witness, in that he did good, and gave us rain from heaven, and fruitful seasons, filling our hearts with food and gladness" (Acts 14:17). Japan is a very beautiful and fertile land, and it is this very bounty with which some Shintoists begin when describing their religion. One of their scholars, Professor Hirai, writing on the theme "The Principles of Shrine Shinto," begins under the subtitle "Kami" and opens with this paragraph:

> Let us quietly look about us on the earth on which we live. There are lovely mountains and rivers, green plains and forests. The salty breezes, blowing in from the oceans rich with treasures, bring about a pleasant, comfortable climate. In the spring the new grass springs forth, and in the autumn the ripening of various fruits and grains is expected. The people have come to feel that this nature surrounding them is held in some great invisible hand. (p. 39)

Here we have confirmation of the very thing Paul was saying about the heathen, that God had left in nature a witness of His beauty and goodness and that the pagan world could not but take notice of Him. But what do they do with Him? Although they begin their myths with a concept of a Highest Being to start things going, and testify that all nature witnesses to the existence of divine power and goodness, they switch their worship to the visible creation, making a god out of the warm and comforting sun, or filling the fields, forests, and mountains with nature spirits and worshiping the spirits of their deceased ancestors. God simply melts into His creation, and the cosmos is deified. The Creator fades away and the creature is substituted for Him (Rom. 1:25). Man makes himself a sovereign deity both by assuming the authority to choose his own gods, gods of his own imagination, and by worshiping the spirits of his own human ancestors as gods. The Shintoist makes a little box, puts it on a shelf, calling it the *kamidana* or god shelf, claims his ancestors' spirits live within, and says, "Here are my gods!" The Creator is pushed out of the sphere of his life and fades away. A short time after the Pacific War, I recall receiving a letter from a young woman who wanted me to put her in touch with a "pen pal," someone who would write to her in English. She said, "I want to learn about Christianity and God. Sometimes I know He *is*, but at other times He fades far away."

The Shintoist scholar and his followers start with the goodness of nature as a witness to the existence of "some great invisible hand" behind it all, and then they bury God in His creation and worship and serve the creature. The Christian missionary needs to go and say to them, "He who has made the warm sun, the lovely mountains and plains, the salty breeze and the life-giving rain, He who makes the rice to grow and gives you your children is the one you have hidden by perverting His witness to you, by crediting creaturely or imagined spirits with this goodness, and worshiping and serving the creature rather than the Creator. Now God would have you turn from these vanities and worship Him through His Son whom He has sent to be our Saviour, and this is the One whom we have come to tell you about." The Father has not left Himself without a witness, and although the heathen have perverted its testimony, the missionary has here a point of contact, a starting point of attack, for this ministry of the Word of conviction of the Holy Spirit and reconciliation of the Son.

Example: Buddhism

Now let us consider what the Buddhists have done with God. If Shintoism can be called an optimistic religion, Buddhism may better be described as a pessimistic one. It originated in India when a young prince, S'akyamuni Gautama (566-486 B.C.), disgusted by the selfish, immoral, evil world around him, sought a way to rise above it rather than be overwhelmed by it. Neither an appeal for help to the polytheistic gods of the common people nor the hope for a better reincarnation for his soul into this world of the Brahman religion appealed to him. He retired into the mountains, deserting his young wife and son, and spent years in meditation. Finally, he claimed one day to receive the light he sought, and from then on he went to the world as the Enlightened One, that is the Buddha.

What was this light? In essence, it was the idea that desire was the cause of all evil and that salvation lay in conquering it. It could only be, and had to be, conquered by a man's own efforts. To seek help from gods or one God was a vain attempt to escape one's responsibilities. No gods existed; there was no personal God. Nor was there any soul, for if all desire was evil, the desire to save one's soul and see it attain a heavenly paradise was a mere seductive illusion that kept the evil of desire stirring in one's heart. So, too, was the Brahman concept of reincarnations—through a transmigration cycle, into a station commensurate with the merits or demerits accumulated in life—all fantasy, he said. All is a great One, like a great ocean, in which individual ripples or waves spring up for a few moments of history and fall back into the great oneness again. What is transmigrated is not a soul but one's karma, his desert [dē·zert´] or merit, which the law of cause and effect demands to be fulfilled in some other individual life. Man's goal must thus be to conquer desire and put an end to this terrible chain of births and deaths stemming from the necessity of the karma of the deceased being fulfilled in the lives of the living until all desire is conquered, and there is no karma requiring satisfaction. The way to this conquest is the Noble Eightfold Path, in which one by one the fetters of sinful desire are overcome and *Nirvana*, "the highest condition of moral rest," is reached in this life. Then when death comes, there is no more karma to be reborn, but only a melting into the great oneness.

This teaching of S'akyamuni, the founder of Buddhism, was a wholesale assault on the image of God in man. It was a carefully worked out attempt, based on the complete suppression of man's inner self-consciousness of himself as having an immortal soul and of his God-consciousness witnessing to the existence of God. It is perhaps the earliest recorded attempt of man to produce a complete suppression of God, a sophisticated atheism. How did it fare in its journey through history?

The history of Buddhism has been one of a long conflict between the original teaching of Buddha—denying the existence of both a personal God and the immortal soul of man, maintained only by the most philosophic of its leaders—and the beliefs of the common Buddhist, layman and priest, which remorselessly come to the surface because of the seed of religion within them, that man has a soul and that there is divine power available to those who pray. As Buddhism came to the common man, and crossed the centuries and continents, man's inner God-consciousness and soul-consciousness moved him to remold and reshape this religion, to make it less in conflict with this inner knowledge. Still, he suppressed and distorted the truth from which the urge sprang. Buddhism came to Japan in the 6th century A.D., by way of China where it picked up Confucian concepts of ethics, traces of Taoist dualism, and many polytheistic concepts. Today idols of Buddha are worshiped as a supreme deity and the greatest festival is Obon, the week in which souls are held to return from paradise to earth and then are lighted back with a lantern festival.

There is a great variety of doctrines and sects, some of the strongest of which trace back to two scholars sent by the Japanese emperor to China in the 9th century. That was the period of the decline of Nestorian Christianity in north China. Whether there is any connection or not, from the sects and writings produced by these two men, later, in the early 12th century, sprang a new element of teaching: faith in the efficacious name of Amida Buddha. This idea of faith in Buddha to secure salvation to a Pure Land is now widely prevalent in Japan. The scholars teach that there is no living Buddha to extend help to men but that it is man's invocation of his name, that is, human effort, which saves, but, to the common people, Buddha appears more to be a supreme deity who can hear their prayers and aid them. Thus have they remade Buddhism in Japan and placed Buddha on the throne of God.

The debate between these two views can be seen in the discussions among the scholars, such as the recently published *Living Buddhism in Japan* (Yoshiro), in which the idea of life after death is examined. One scholar maintained that such a belief indeed had very good effects "in calming the mind at death," but still "it cannot be said that such a world exists."

Another replied, "If seeking a world after death is a feeling common to human beings, it must be asked why such a feeling takes place. In other words, the desire to seek it arises because there is a world after death. If there is nothing, it would be impossible even to think about its existence or its form."

A third admitted,

It can be said that the past tendency of Buddhism [in Japan] has been to recognize the soul. When we look back at Buddhist history, however, we find that many things, which are not proper to Buddhism, have become mixed with it. Views of the soul and memorial services to ancestral spirits may be examples of this. How to deal with these matters is an urgent problem, which we modern Buddhists should solve. If we leave Buddhism halfway as it is, it may run off in an unforeseeable direction.

A professor then suggested that the real question was "how to interpret the soul in Buddhism," the inference seeming to be that scholars could go along with the common man's use of the term if they conceived of it but in a figurative sense.

It was then pointed out that Japanese Buddhists have increasingly thought of Buddha as a great deity who watched over them and was ready to help if called upon. Even the great Nichiren, founder of one of the most dynamic of Buddhist sects in Japan in the 12th century "in his old age placed a Buddha opposite him and sought the Pure Land for his future life" in prayer. In modern times, there are many Buddhists who consider themselves to be friends of Buddha through a particular idol of him which they worship daily. The remark was made by one scholar, "Such people are very diligent in their business because they think that the deity is always keeping his eye on them. Accordingly, their trade is prosperous."

Thus, throughout the history of Buddhism, the struggle has gone on between the original, deliberate, philosophical rejection of the existence of God and the human soul, and man's universal consciousness of God and of his soul stemming from his creation in the image of God and God's revelation of Himself in nature. Men unceasingly try to suppress this truth, and satisfy its promptings with a distortion of it, in creature and spirit worship, but they cannot destroy it. God has preserved His witness to them. They have sought to hide Him away from themselves, to cover Him completely with substitute gods so that He cannot be seen, or even to deny that he exists apart from the temporal universe about us, but they cannot escape Him. His "speech" is ever ringing in their ears as Paul and the psalmist have pointed out.

It is the missionary's task to point this out to them. He must tell them what they have been doing and that their incessant search for more satisfactory worship, without satisfaction, is evidence that they have not been looking to the truth, the true God of creation, about whom the missionary has come to tell them. It is our blessed privilege to tell them the good news: that the God of heaven has made them in His image, with this inner longing to worship Him, which they have been suppressing and distorting; and that He has now sent His Son (and, to them, the ambassadors of His Son) with the message that He will forgive their sins and idolatry if they will repent of them and turn from their idols to serve the living and true God, through His Son who died for us and rose again from the dead. They are capable of "hearing" this Word, this special revelation, with a natural understanding if we carefully explain it, because God has seen to it that they have never been outside the hearing of His "speech," of His general revelation.

When they understand it in this way, with less misinterpretation, some will say, "This is not what we thought it was. We don't want it." Others may say, "We want to think it over some more and hear more about it." But some, God's elect, will, in His time, have the eyes of their spiritual understanding opened by the regenerating power of the Holy Spirit. They will say, "This is the truth. This is the message of the true God and Savior." They will repent and be saved. It is the missionary's task to work for and to pray for such results as he preaches.

Man's Moral Consciousness

When we go on to consider what Japan's two ancient religions have done with man's ineradicable moral-consciousness, we come to the same sad story. In Shintoism there is a clear recognition of both good and evil, and that man ought to do good and not evil. However, it is accompanied by an incessant effort to break down the difference by making the desires of man's heart the criterion of good. To quote again from the Shinto scholar in *The Kami Way*,

> The soul of man is good. This is the kami world. Evil then cannot originate in man or in this world. It is an intruder. Evil comes from without . . . . While man's soul is good, the flesh and senses readily succumb to temptation. Man commits evil because he has lost, has been deprived of the capacity for, normal action. In modern Shinto, there is no fixed and unalterable moral code. Good and evil are relative. The meaning and value of an action depends on its circumstances, motives, purpose, time, place, etc. Generally speaking, however, man's heart must be sincere . . . . Sin and evil are caused by evil spirits, which must be exorcised. Therefore, it is necessary to distinguish clearly between good and evil. That by which good and evil can be distinguished is the soul of man. This distinction is made possible by the help of the kami.

Thus although the necessity of distinguishing between good and evil is acknowledged, the natural man of the Shintoist tries to smooth this over by declaring that good and evil are relative to what a man sincerely thinks and wants.

Because men's souls are held to be originally pure, as descendent from the gods, one hears much about "common sense" among Shintoist-influenced Japanese. Man's "common sense" is his guide to right and wrong. So long as he can keep sincere, his judgments will be good. If one sins it is a mistake and can be remedied. Sin, like dust on the hand, can be removed by the ceremonial cleansing water of the shrine, and man can be restored to his original pure nature and capacity to do good.

With these opiates the Shintoist tries to calm his moral-consciousness before a history in which the "common sense" way led to grossly immoral standards, reckless taking of one's neighbor's life and wife, and great disregard for truthfulness. The Shintoist man has found himself utterly impotent to control the lusts of his own heart and he is also utterly without excuse for he has claimed that his heart was pure and capable of right living. He has suppressed the truth about himself and his need. He needs to hear the missionary's message from God concerning the truth: that "the heart of man is deceitful above all things and desperately wicked"; that there is a holy God; that sin is violation of His Holy standards; and that he must repent, therefore, and be baptized in the name of Jesus Christ for the remission of sins.

In Buddhism, too, we see man's clear recognition of a distinction between right and wrong, good and evil, and his effort to reduce sin to that which man can himself conquer. Buddha taught that all desire was evil but that man could follow the Eightfold Noble Path and conquer all desire. In Japan, Pure Land Buddhism teaches "that human beings are by nature sinful." Man "cannot but commit sin. Furthermore, he cannot be at peace in it. Religion must play the role of solving such a conflict. Seeking only divine favor is often seen in new religions, but this is not true faith."

Zen Buddhists teach, "If one repents, sins go away like dew or frost in the light of the sun." One Buddhist scholar defines sin by saying, "Sin in Buddhism seems to mean the absence of harmony." He then admits that due to this, some Buddhists in the past have declared, "Even when one commits adultery, if he is not attached to it, it does not constitute a sin." Here again then we see men acknowledging the truth about their sinful nature, but following it with a degeneration of the concept of sin and an elevation of man's ability to cope with it. There is no concept of sin as defiance of a holy God. Further, if disaster or blessing is unrelated to the plan of an all-wise divine being, and only based on an inheritance of someone's good or ill karma, then only a fatalistic and pessimistic view can ensue. The belief that all desire is evil stultifies all progress: the history of Buddhist Asia. The stark pessimism of this present evil world and the hope of a better reincarnation in another life tempt men to suicide, one of the chief causes of death in Japan. Surely here we have one of Satan's masterpieces: using sinful man's suppression of the truth within him and getting him so to distort it that he believes salvation lies in self destruction, when after death there can be only judgment!

The lesson we can learn then from elenctics is that the heathen religions bear out well the truth of God's Word concerning God's revelation of Himself to all men in nature and in man himself. It behooves the missionary of God's special revelation to understand the pagan religion that he may better be able to expose to the non-Christian his own inner rebellion against the God who has not left Himself without a witness to him; praying always that the Holy Spirit will bring the conviction of sin, repentance, and faith in our Lord and Savior Jesus Christ that is absolutely essential for salvation.

Questions for Study and Discussion

1. What is *elenctics*? How does it apply to missionary work?
2. What has the Shintoist done with his God-consciousness?
3. What have the Buddhists done with God?
4. What is the missionary's duty in the field of elenctics?
5. What have Japan's two ancient religions done with man's ineradicable moral-consciousness?
6. What chief lesson do we learn from a study of elenctics?

6

Identification and Accommodation

The subject we have before us is one that faces the missionary with many puzzling problems. To what extent should he identify himself with the life of the people to whom he goes to minister? When does such identification become unjustifiable accommodation, even sinful compromise? These two terms, *identification* and *accommodation*, perhaps do not automatically cover the areas in which adaptation is justifiable or not justifiable, but I think we can use them to convey the idea of this distinction. Accommodation can convey the idea of unacceptable compromise, of an adaptation to customs and practices that are basically foreign to the gospel in that they limit or bring something of paganism into it. Identification, on the other hand, connotes more of a making oneself at one with the people in their daily life, to whatever extent this is feasible. Identification should help them make the complete break with pagan religious ideas that the gospel requires, not help them accommodate Christianity to these views and practices. We can, therefore, choose to use these terms to bear this distinction.

The problem of course arises when we ask, when is it lawful identification and when is it unlawful accommodation? This problem must have arisen many times as the early Christians came out of heathenism and began to lead their lives in a pagan culture. Indeed, we see it in the repeated warning to "keep yourselves from idols" (1 John 5:21; 1 Cor. 10:14). Apparently, the line between lawful identification and unlawful accommodation was an easy one to overstep. If we look at one New Testament illustration that crops up several times, however, we may get some help in determining criteria that may assist us in drawing the line between the two.

When Gentiles began to be converted to Christ, problems arose that necessitated the first assembly of church officers at the Jerusalem Conference, recorded in Acts 15, to cope with them. The conference's conclusions were then sent out to the churches, that the Gentiles did not have to be circumcised but that they should "abstain from meats offered to idols, and from blood, and from things strangled and from fornication." Here we have *proscriptions*, which seem to deal with religious, practical, and moral considerations. It is the first proscription, concerning meats offered to idols, however, which seems to have caused some to feel (later, however) that it should have been put in the category of a harmless practice rather than that of a forbidden one. We find Paul bringing it up for lengthy consideration a few years later in 1 Corinthians 8. The question here is not deliberately participating with pagans in their idolatrous religious exercises. That is forbidden elsewhere and is the presupposition behind the present consideration. "Be ye not unequally yoked together with unbelievers. . . what agreement hath the temple of God with idols? Come from them and be ye separate" (2 Cor. 6:14, 17).

The problem is what to do with things already used in idolatrous worship and that are still the symbols of idolatrous worship to some. The position Paul takes here does not allow for the ignoring of the decision of the Jerusalem Council. Rather, he upholds it because of the almost sure possibility of putting a stumbling block in someone's path if it is ignored. He even warns against eating in a restaurant on the temple grounds, where everything is dedicated to the service of the idols, lest the example lead someone to ruin.

But in 1 Corinthians 10, Paul seems to carry the argument against eating things sacrificed to idols beyond that of the possible ill effects it may have on others to an apparent condemnation based on the nature of the thing and the ill effect it may have on the participator himself. In verse 14 he warns, "Flee from idolatry." Then he cites two illustrations as background for the conclusion he is to draw. The Christian communion service is a fellowshiping with Christ (vv. 16-17). Next, in verse 18, the Jews eating the temple sacrifices understand that they are partaking of all that is symbolized by the altar. To them it means a communion with God. Is it different with the heathen? Not that there is any reality to the idol, Paul repeats, but that behind the idol there are demons. It is to these the Gentiles are really sacrificing, and their offerings are a symbol of their communion. The Christian cannot fellowship with demons, nor can he participate at a table where demon offerings are being made (vv. 19-21). The one who thinks he is strong enough to do this without harm is thinking that he is stronger than God, because God has forbidden it (v. 22). Then verses 23, 27-28 read:

> All things are lawful for me, but all things are not expedient: all things are lawful for me, but all things edify not. . . . If any of them that believe not bid you to a feast, and ye be disposed to go; whatsoever is set before you, eat, asking no question for conscience sake. But if any man say unto you, This is offered in sacrifice unto idols, eat not for his sake that shewed it, and for conscience sake: for the earth is the Lord's and the fullness thereof.

If anything has a very loose or distant connection with an idolatrous symbol this is not of vital concern, unless another points out the connection as something to be avoided (v. 28).

As the century drew to a close, we see that this matter of eating or refraining from food sacrificed to idols was a key test of loyalty to Christ. John mentions it in connection with the sins of two of the seven churches in Revelation, condemning the church of Thyatira for listening to one who led them "to commit fornication, and to eat things sacrificed to idols" (Rev. 2:20).

Even in the passage where Paul warns against any conduct that might compromise one's own or another believer's testimony, however, he does go on to indicate that he himself practiced a measure of identification. In 1 Corinthians 9:20-22 we read,

> And unto the Jews I became as a Jew, that I might gain the Jews; to them that are under the law, as under the law; that I might gain them that are under the

law; to them that are without law as without law (although not lawless toward God but committed to Christ's law) that I might gain them that are without law. To the weak became I as weak, that I might gain the weak; I am made all things to all men, that I might by all means save some.

From these considerations, I think we can draw a helpful criterion in assisting us to distinguish between lawful identification and unlawful accommodation. Briefly stated it would be this: In religion, separation; in life, identification. By this we mean that whenever there is a direct or close and well-known association with heathen religion in a pagan cultural practice, then the Christian must be separate from it. On the other hand, when it is a matter of a Christian identifying himself with the life of the heathen, where such close religious associations do not exist, such identification is lawful and exemplary in order to win them to the gospel.

The objection will perhaps be raised, however, that all the heathen do is related to their religion, that heathen religion is a total world-and-life view as is Christianity. Although this is in a sense true, there are very different degrees of that relation. Not all that they do is related directly or immediately to their religion. Many of their cultural practices, having to do with etiquette, dress, diet, or house construction, may have long since lost their religious significance, whereas certain aspects still prominently maintain it. It is where that obvious religious aspect exists that the Christian is warned to be careful. If an effort is being made to carry over into Christianity something from pagan symbolism; to make the break between the two seem less sharp; to maintain some seeming continuing connection; to make Christianity more palatable to the non-Christian, by lessening its uniqueness; then a form of syncretism and, therefore, unlawful accommodation is in view. But now, let us consider some specific illustrations of this problem in order to become more familiar with it and to know how to face it.

Lawful Identification

First, let us consider the matter of lawful identification. The area of language is one where the new missionary will probably first face this problem. The missionary cannot invent a new language in which to present his message; he must use the one of the people. Yet working in the area of religion, he will learn to watch for words that have a general or generic significance and those that have a special significance, peculiarly related to a specific religion.

The word *God* may serve as an example. When the first missionaries went to China they had a choice between *Shen* and *Shang Ti*. Shen was the generic word for god but, like Chinese and Japanese nouns, could have either a plural or singular meaning, depending on the context. To this extent it is similar to the Hebrew word *Elohim*. However, in China, Shen to the common people had a predominantly polytheistic significance. Shang Ti, on the other hand, although used by Confucius to refer to the highest deity, had become the particular name of the deity worshiped by the emperor as the high priest of the people at the Temple of Heaven and Altar of Heaven in Peking. The name of this deity had a very august rating in China, which was not the case with Shen. Thus the early missionaries chose Shang Ti and it appeared as the translation for God in the first Bibles.

But was that a wise choice? Later missionaries came to feel it was not, and eventually the word Shen was put in its place. They found that when they used the specific name Shang Ti, all the specific characteristics of that deity and its worship carried over in the minds of the people to the living and true God, whereas when the general term Shen was used, such specific connotations were less apt to be present, and it was easier to present the God whom they meant. Thus, as Paul when he went to the Greeks chose the generic term *Theos* to translate Elohim, so they turned to the generic term *En*. In Japan, likewise, the generic term *Kami* was chosen in spite of its widespread polytheistic use.

A similar problem arose in the choice of a word for *logos* in John 1:1. Some advocated the use of the word *dao* meaning way or principle, but with a highly honored specifically religious meaning in the Taoist religion; the divine world order, the principle behind all. This was chosen for use in the Chinese Bible, although it was rejected in Japan in favor of the ordinary word for "word," *katoba*. In Japan, these two Chinese ideographs together, *Shen tao* pronounced Shinto, have been used as the name of the Shinto religion, which claims to present the way of the gods. It was felt that *tao* or *to* carried over to Christ some of the pagan concepts and that a literal translation, which was free from these and, therefore, could be explained in its own context, was much better.

A modern language problem in Japan today concerns the translation of the future tense. The Japanese language has no single future tense corresponding to the English or Greek future.

They have a form used for a great variety of events more or less likely to take place in the future, called by some of their leading grammarians a probability form. When they refer, however, to something that they expect almost certainly to take place in the future, they use the present tense. For instance, the arrival of trains in Japan is very punctual, and almost invariably one uses the present tense when referring to times of arrival. The probability form would almost certainly infer an unscheduled event likely to delay the train. On the other hand, weather forecasting is highly problematical and radio announcers forecast in the probability form. Yet in the colloquial version of the Bible of the Japan Bible Society, the probability form is used of the promises and prophecies of the Word of God. The translators reported that it was their hope to establish this probability form as the real, true future tense of the Japanese language, a rather optimistic view considering that the Christians of Japan using this Bible represent about one fourth of one percent of the population! Far more likely is it that the uninformed reader will receive the impression that in Christianity things are as uncertain as they are in Buddhism. It is the influence of Buddhism that probably accounts for the lack of a true future tense. Here is almost certainly a case of improper language identification. The missionary to a new field certainly must be acutely aware of this problem.

The area of etiquette is another in which the missionary can properly practice identification. Polite consideration is understood in every country and appreciated, but in some lands the method of expressing it is different. There are lands where a visiting male missionary would greatly embarrass the woman of the home if he stepped back and insisted she go through the door before he did. In Japan, it would be the essence of inconsiderateness to wear one's shoes into the home of a friend. To learn and practice the customs and manner of greeting, sincerely, and not as if one considered them foolish, is an important part of identification with the life of the people for the gospel's sake. There are certain customs, however, that cannot be followed because of their obvious religious connection, even if one runs the hazard of being considered discourteous, such as declining to bow before the household god shelf, or to burn incense before a coffin. If the omission is obviously noticed, the missionary may have an opportunity to give a testimony to the fact that men need to make a clear distinction between their relation to their deceased ancestors and the Creator, the living God. We respect the memory of our ancestors, but we worship only the true God.

The areas of dress, diet, and housing are others where identification can be considered. In the early days of missions, missionaries to new fields often practiced almost complete identification with the people in these areas. Because the Western standard was in almost all cases scientifically more practical and useful, they found that soon the more progressive natives were learning and practicing the Western way to some extent. In this modern day of worldwide travel and ready availability almost anywhere of a host of Western-style goods, the need for this kind of identification is greatly lessened. Even the missionary to the Aucas in the wild Amazon jungles has access to Western food and clothing to some extent due to the airplane.

The problem of identification in these matters probably has more to do with levels of wealth. In most lands the missionary's dollar goes far and could enable him to live on a level quite a bit above the ordinary native. How much then should the missionary sacrifice in order to live nearer the native level? Further, with what level should he compare his own standard of living to that of a farmer, storekeeper, office worker, teacher, or business executive? I have known missionaries who have tried to live at the farmer level or office clerk level, but I have not noticed that this brought them any special consideration. In most lands, the missionary is considered a teacher, an honorable level where a standard of living higher than the ordinary one is expected. On the whole, it is the excessively beautiful or modern home and the almost exclusive use of imported foods that are likely to cause criticism.

Should the missionary use a car? This will almost certainly put him in a class by himself in Asian or African lands. If it adds greatly to his efficiency and the substantial increase of the number and variety of services he can render, then there is no reason why he cannot. He can point out that it is a necessary part of his equipment even as farm animals and equipment are to the farmer or a store to a storekeeper, but in that case he had better prove his point by using his car for something more than his own pleasure driving!

"All things to all men" (1 Cor. 9:22) does not necessarily mean giving up that which will make one a more efficient servant. One's attitude is of the utmost importance in this matter of identification. If the missionary's attitude is one of inner contempt for the way of life of the nationals, it will soon be detected and resented. The defeat of such an attitude, in spite of whatever discrepancy there exists between the two ways of living, is essential. As for the difference, one writer has observed, "The wall about the compound does not make so much difference if the gate is always open to receive those who wish to come in." The missionary will want to identify himself with the life of the people to some extent to be acceptable, but in some regards, where health or morals are involved, he will find it undesirable. Distinguishing himself from their way of life in such areas should serve to help them to an improved way.

Unlawful Accommodation

But now let us consider the other and perhaps more difficult problem: that of unlawful accommodation. One of the most difficult situations in this area occurs when the government requires as an act of patriotism what is still an act of pagan religious exercise (the government trying to make it more palatable for Christians by declaring it to be patriotism only). This became a very difficult problem early in Japan missions.

In 1890, the government, in order to unite the people around the emperor, and to hold them to the traditional manner of thought, introduced the Imperial Rescript and portrait into the schools. On certain special occasions a school assembly was held, the Rescript was read as a message from the God-Emperor, and the students were ordered to bow in worship before his unveiled portrait. These ceremonies at first caused a great stir in Christian circles with real opposition being offered, but the government was adamant. To make it easier for Christians, the religious bureau released a statement that these ceremonies were not religious but only patriotic. Several considerations, however, showed them to be of a polytheistic nature, and, therefore, religious in the Christian meaning of the word. The Rescript statement opened with a reference to the "ancestors," but the Chinese ideographs used were for the mythological deities of Shintoism. The next set of ideograph used referred to the human ancestors of the emperors. Further, it spoke of "the Imperial Throne coeval with heaven and earth," and the "way here set forth is . . . infallible in all ages and true in all places." To a Christian, these can be nothing but the religious concepts of a primitive polytheism. A government new release could not change their religious nature.

Still further, was it not unlawful compromise for a Christian to bow in worship before the portrait of the emperor, even though the student might have no worshipful feeling in his heart?

The answer lies in the second commandment, where it is declared, 'Thou shalt not make unto thee any. . . likeness of anything that is in heaven above, or that is in the earth beneath, or that is in the water under the earth. Thou shalt not bow down thyself to them, nor serve them' (Ex. 20:4-5). The Hebrew word—translated here as 'bow down' in the English and as *ogamu* (worship) in the Japanese—is *shachah*. The *International Standard Bible Encyclopedia*, in a learned article on the word 'worship,' makes it clear that the root idea of shachah is that of bodily prostration with a view to showing reverence. When it is performed to living men in their presence, where no idea of deity is associated, the Scriptures uniformly recognize the act of prostration or bowing as a legitimate salutation. As an act of worship to the living God, who is Spirit, or as only an act of respect in the presence of a living man, who is spirit and body, created in the image of God, shachah (to worship or bow down before) is correct behavior.

What the Scriptures uniformly condemn, and the second commandment specifically condemns, is the act of bowing, whether merely as an outward act or as one including the inner, emotional, worshipful feeling, towards anything other than living persons, specifically anything made in the "likeness of anything that is in the heaven above, or that is in the earth beneath." The act of bowing, when performed otherwise than as an act of salutation to a living person, is a worshipful act, whether performed from an inner, emotional religious feeling, or simply performed as an outward act without such feeling, according to the Scriptural presentation of the matter.

The three young Hebrew heroes of the third chapter of Daniel obviously so understood it, for if the only *shachah* (bow down or worship) forbidden by the second command was one associated with an inner religious feeling, then they could have bowed down in good conscience knowing that there was no such feeling in their hearts. They well knew, however, that it was the act of bowing itself, which was forbidden, and that to do so would be to "worship the image." Thus apart from the fact that the school bow to the portrait was made to the picture of one who was declared to be a god, and that the bow required was for the students' "profoundest obeisance," of which there could be none deeper in act or inner meaning, apart from these obvious considerations, the fact that the bow was to the material reproduction of a man, should have been reason enough for Christians to classify it in the category of forbidden acts of an idolatrous nature. That they did not do so established the practice of compromise with the national polytheism for three generations of Christians to come, leaving an imprint so deep that even today few churches in Japan have completely extricated themselves from it. This early failure to discern between that which could be rendered "to Caesar" and that which was God's alone resulted in the planting of a seed which within a half century was to bring forth a harvest of destruction in the moral fiber of the Church. (Young, pp. 54-55)

The unlawful accommodation involved in Christians participating in the Rescript ceremonies was a sinful compromise. It had a profound effect on the whole future of Christianity in Japan, conditioning it to have a tolerant attitude toward participation in polytheistic practices up to this very day.

Another situation involving unlawful accommodation concerns Christian use of Shinto Kamidana (god shelves) and Buddhist Butsudan (Buddhist idol altars) in the home. These objects are present in a great majority of Japanese homes for the worship of the ancestors' spirits. The Buddhist altar contains an *ihai* or ancestral tablet in which the names of the ancestors are written. To worship these things would obviously be idolatry, but the argument has been made that they can lawfully be accommodated to Christian use. For instance, one Kyodan pastor (United Church of Japan) made this recommendation in 1951:

Then what will this writer recommend? The real sense of the Butsudan comes from the fact that there is an image or picture enshrined in it. Thus if we take these away we cannot call it a Butsudan. Therefore we have only to return these to the original temple with some offering money. Next we must consider the "ihai." The Buddhist names of the deceased being written on the front side, these must be removed and the "ihai" turned around, so that we can see the other side on which are written the dates of the dead. If we go further and remodel the inside of the Butsudan by setting up a cross and a Bible there we can have a fine Christian holy place. Thus the spirit of Christianity can be breathed into Japanese Buddhists who have made Buddha images but neglected to put a real spirit in them.

What is the objective here? Is it to achieve a sort of syncretism between pagan and Christian symbols, to make the difference between the two less apparent? Such a motive is an unworthy one and the method entirely unjustifiable. Hope for the heathen lies in their recognition of the uniqueness of Christianity, and a complete break with those objects which were the very symbols of their substitution of the worship of the spirits of deceased creaturely men for the living Creator. The idea that the presence of a Christian symbol like a cross in a pagan idol box can sanctify it is reminiscent of the Israelitish superstition that they could make God serve their purposes by taking out the Ark of the Covenant onto the battlefield. The call in 2 Corinthians 6 is for complete separation from such things. Paul's warning in 1 Corinthians 10:22 needs to be heeded: "Do we provoke the Lord to jealousy? Are we stronger than He?"

A somewhat similar recommendation to the above pastors also came from a missionary in Japan concerning another matter, the Obon Festival. This is a Buddhist festival held each summer in which the spirits of the dead are welcomed back to their homes for a few days. Christians in Japan are under great pressure to participate in this pagan religious observance to show their filial piety. Thus this missionary recommended that the Obon Festival be declared a Christian "All Saints Day" so that Christians too could observe the day. He wrote:

> The process of adjusting Christian religious practices to Japanese culture is already taking place . . . . Because of the desire to pay respects to the dead, it would be an easy matter for the Christian Church to develop an Obon (festival of the dead) observance. Many Christians have to return to their native place at this time, help clean up the cemetery and participate in a Buddhist service or they will not be considered filial by their relatives . . . . Japanese people will adjust their Christian worship and practices to their old faiths.

Such an adjustment between polytheistic faith and Christian faith is sinful syncretism. How will the heathen ever learn the distinctive nature of the Christian faith, as the one, true, revealed religion of the Living God? How will they recognize that He alone is worthy of worship and that He forbids all efforts to communicate with the souls of deceased men, whose destinies He holds in the palm of His hand? They cannot if such schemes are worked out to lessen the antithesis between Christianity and polytheism.

But let us mention one more illustration. According to Buddhist funeral rites, there are certain days following the funeral when special memorial services for the dead should take place to ensure the comfortable repose of the deceased's soul in paradise. One of the most important of these days is the first anniversary of the death. To fail to hold such a service is considered by the heathen as gross disinterest in filial piety. Accordingly, to avoid the stigma ensuing, many Christians advocated holding Christian services in the home on that day to which the heathen relatives are also invited. The justification is that this furnishes a good opportunity to give a Christian witness to the unbelieving relatives. The results over the years, however, show otherwise. The actual result has been that the Buddhist relatives are simply confirmed in their belief in the universal acceptance of the idea that the souls of the dead can be comforted by the religious worship of the living, and in the similarity of Buddhist and Christian belief on this point. Further evidence of this lies in the fact that when some Christians tried to get away from the close identification with Buddhist practice by holding the memorial service on some other day than that prescribed by Buddhist ritual, the nonbelievers showed no interest in the service and failed to come. Since Christians did not need the service, there was no use for it. The weakening nature of this kind of accommodation is also seen in that many Christians have shown a definite reluctance and uneasiness about shifting the day to one not prescribed by Buddhist tradition, indicating, as Paul said, that "their conscience being weak is defiled" (1 Cor. 8:7). Such accommodations have shown to be harmful in the long run.

In conclusion, the principle we need to keep in mind is: "In religion, separation; in life, identification." The uniqueness of our revealed faith need not trouble us as we seek to spread the dominion of our Lord. The record of the missionary activity of Rome in medieval times as it accommodated itself in the East to the Oriental religions and to the north with European pagan practices, and as it continued this policy of accommodation at the beginning of the modern era in South America, the Philippines and Japan, should be a warning to all. History has shown that it is those who have most zealously maintained that uniqueness, in love, for the gospel's sake, who have been instrumental in establishing the strongest churches among the nations.

Questions for Study and Discussion

1. Define the terms "identification" and "accommodation" as they relate to foreign missions.

2. Demonstrate from Scripture how Paul avoided accommodation with heathen practices but identified himself with heathen people.

3. Name some areas in which the missionary must make a choice between what is unlawful accommodation and what is lawful identification.

4. To what extent should a missionary identify himself with the people to whom he ministers?

5. Describe a historic example of unlawful accommodation.

6. What does the phrase "In religion, separation; in life, identification" mean to you?

Church, State, and Missions

7

"There seems to be little alternative for a true Christian than to follow the teachings of Peter . . . who refused to compromise Christian truth or discontinue group worship and was ready to suffer the consequence."

Throughout the long history of civilization, the overlapping of religion and state has been the ordinary, not the extraordinary, condition. Ever since the conversion of the Roman emperor Constantine, this has largely been true of the relation between church and state as well, apart from some notable exceptions, chiefly in North America, during the last two centuries. Even today, most of the great churches of Europe are still state churches, although the ties between the two in real practice are more formal than actual.

In non-Christian lands, however, the native religion and state grew up together. The foundation of the state rested on the ideology of its religion, as it was considered a sort of hands and feet of the state. Thus in many of them, and this was certainly true of pre-war Japan, religion and state were considered inseparable, the national polity being based on the religious beliefs. As missionaries went to such lands with the Christian message to found churches, inevitably vexing problems arose between them and the demands of the state, and in some cases serious persecution arose as a result. In the following discussion, we will look at some of these problems, particularly by illustrating them from the uneasy church-state relationships in Japan today, to see what we can learn to help us understand the problems arising through the interaction of church, state, and missions, and how to cope with them.

When we speak of the church here we are thinking primarily of the organized Christian church as an institution, and only of the church as an organism of individual believers when specific reference to such is made. The authority of the state is derived from God, resting on His common grace, and sin-conditioned. The state is limited to its sphere by the operation of divine authority in the other spheres of church, society, family, and individual, by the necessity of acting according to just and lawful principles, and by being external in character, having to do with the regulation of outward conduct rather than inner attitude.

Religious freedom in the framework of this discussion will be presented as the right of self-determination of religion, including creed, worship, practice, policy, organization, proclamation, and effort to win others, as well as the freedom to abstain from contrary practices. This freedom is God-given and is reflected in the dignity of the human person as God's image bearer. Since we are to set the problem of the relationship between church and state, which in a non-Christian land is stated in terms of religion and state, in the setting of Japan, we need to understand the background of government in Japan.

Example: Japan

The situation in Japan, of a nation changing from a pre-war military despotism to a post-war constitutional democracy, furnishes interesting material for the study of the church-state problem. The changing Japanese scene is illustrative of a change taking place in other mission lands as well. Let us begin, then, by considering briefly what the pre-war relationship between state, church, and missions was in Japan.

In the decade before the war, Japan was a constitutional monarchy that had become a religio-militaristic despotism. One of the early edicts following the Meiji Restoration of 1868 had declared, "The worship of the gods and regard for [*Shinto*] ceremonies are the great properties of the empire and the fundamental principles of national polity [*kokutai*] and education . . . . Thus the Way of the unity of religion and government [*saisei itchi*] shall be revived." This policy had come to on full fruition in the 1930s with the significance of the inseparability of religion and state being pressed to their full implications.

In spite of the Meiji Constitution, which seemed to guarantee freedom of religion, the avowed unity of government and the Shinto religion, whenever pressed, made any true freedom for Christianity impossible. The actual statement in the constitution, which was supposed to guarantee religious freedom, declared, "Japanese subjects shall, within the limits not prejudicial to peace and order, and not antagonistic to their duties as subjects, enjoy freedom of religious belief." The great potential for trouble lay in the phrase "their duties as subjects." Some of these "duties" were enunciated in the Imperial Rescript on Education promulgated that year as the basis of the educational system. It presented the Shinto ideology by connecting the origin of Japan to the activity of the mythological, ancestral gods and demanded "filial affection" to them as well as to their divine human descendants. This "filial affection" to these "divine ancestors" was declared to be "our national polity" (*kokutai*). The children were called upon to show their support of it by bowing in low obeisance to the Emperor's portrait when it was exhibited before them on special, ceremonial occasions. In the early Roman Empire, when the state pressed such claims and demanded obeisance from the Christian church, resistance and persecution followed. What happened in Japan?

The small church in Japan took the line of non-resistance, placating its conscience with the view that all of this was only of patriotic and not religious significance. This was in spite of the fact that the rescript was polytheistic to the core, declaring that the "Imperial Throne [is] coeval with heaven and earth," and that "the Way here set forth is . . . infallible in all ages and true in all places." Further, the church closed its eyes to the requirements of the second commandment in allowing its covenant children to bow to the picture of a man, and later allowing them to be led out to the Shinto shrines to bow there also.

When the enforced shrine visitation first began to be pressed, the National Christian Council (NCC) of Japan did raise an objection. This body of cooperating Japanese churches and missions issued a statement in 1930 declaring:

> To treat the Shinto shrines, which from of old have been religious, as nonreligious has been unreasonable. The shrines of Shrine [state] Shinto are actually engaged in religious functions. This has given rise to much confusion. Fur-

thermore, recently the Government in its effort to foster religious faith has promoted worship at the shrines of Shrine Shinto and even made it compulsory. This is clearly contrary to the policy that Shrine Shinto is nonreligious.

In 1936, however, as fanatical Shinto militarists gained control of the government and shrine participation was pressed with great vigor, the NCC reversed its position and declared, "We accept the definition of the government that the Shinto shrine is nonreligious." The Japanese church as a whole approved this declaration, although a few individual pastors and missionaries refused to accept this verdict, even closing their Bible or theological schools rather than letting their young people do either *jinja sampai* (shrine obeisance) or *kyujo yohai* (distant worship towards the Emperor's palace).

The following comment of a missionary in Manchuria facing these things is worth noting here: "The fact that the magistrate may, by a stroke of official legerdemain [sleight of hand], declare that ceremonies which include priesthood and altar, sacrifices and prayers, possess no religious significance, does not alter the situation in the slightest; it is not what the magistrate says about such ceremonies, but what they plainly are in themselves, that constitutes their inherent immorality and incompatibility with Christian practice" (Vos, p. 8).

The pagan Shinto-militaristic state, which had succeeded in leading the church into one compromise after another, did not stop until it forced all the churches into the one United Church of Christ in Japan (*Nihon Kirisuto Kyodan*) in 1941, and all religions, Christian, Shinto, and Buddhist, into one Religious Association in 1944. In 1949, when the NCC gave its official explanation to the World Council of Churches' conference in Bangkok as to why the church did not give more resistance to the claims of the pagan state in Japan, they stated, "There seemed only two alternatives for the church to follow, either to clash with the militaristic regime at the expense of complete dissolution of the churches and even martyrdom, or to suffer together with their fellow countrymen in perseverance and sacrifice. The sense of national solidarity led our church people to choose the latter position" (Young, p. 69). As this statement indicates, the church in Japan, rather than choosing the course of loyalty to Christ and subsequent persecution and possible martyrdom, chose to identify itself with the course of the pagan state.

The end of the war brought fantastic changes to Japan. How did these affect the relationship among church, state, and missions? Modern Japan is comprised of a nation of over 94 million people (1962), living on four main islands whose land area is comparable to California. It is now both a constitutional monarchy and a parliamentary democracy. Through the initiative of the Supreme Commander for the Allied Powers (General MacArthur), a new constitution was prepared and adopted by the government. For the first time in Japan's history, the people of Japan were given an unequivocal guarantee of religious freedom. The actual words of Article 20 of the new constitution declare, "Freedom of religion is guaranteed to all. No religious organization shall receive any privileges from the State, nor exercise any political authority. No person shall be compelled to take part in any religious act, celebration, rite or practice." This constitution also commits the nation to pacifism by stating in Article 9, "The Japanese people forever renounce war as a sovereign right of the nation and the threat or use of force as a means of settling international disputes. In order to accomplish the aim of the preceding sentence, land, sea, and air forces, as well as other war potential, will never be maintained." This clause has been circumvented to some extent, for Japan today has a small army, navy, and air force, which are called National Self-Defense Forces. Constitutional law is never any stronger than the desire of those whose duty it is to enforce it.

The church in Japan is comprised primarily of the *Nihon Kiristo Kyodan*, the United Church of Christ in Japan, from which large numbers have withdrawn since the war but which claims a membership of about 175,000. The total fragment of the population that would carry the name "Christian" in any sense would be less than 450,000, about half of one percent. Of these, the Protestants would number about 300,000, just about one quarter of one percent. This church is primarily under the sway of liberal and neoorthodox theology. The National Christian Council is again activated and is comprised of the N.K. Kyodan, the Baptist Churches (Southern and Northern), the Episcopalians, the Lutherans, the Salvation Army, the Korean Church in Japan, and the YM and YWCA, representing a total of some 237,000 members. Socialism is the predominant political ideology amongst the Christians of these churches.

There are many smaller, evangelical Christian groups, however, working outside of the National Christian Council. Their membership has been estimated as high as 90,000 with perhaps 60 percent of this number representing the product of new, post-war evangelical missionaries.

Missions in Japan today are represented by some 125 different Protestant organizations. This large number reflects the divisions in the Protestant churches of the Western world as well as their great concern to see pagan Japan brought under the influence of the Christian gospel. There are now some 2,500 Protestant missionaries, including their wives and an equal number of Roman Catholic priests and nuns working in every area in Japan. Three different Protestant missionary fellowships fairly accurately reflect three different reactions to the confused condition of Protestantism throughout the world. The oldest of these is the pre-war organization called the Fellowship of Christian Missionaries, representing perhaps some 350 missionaries. Its attitude towards the theological position of their members is latitudinarian, the extremes of liberalism, neoorthodoxy, and evangelical conservatism being represented. Their viewpoint is frequently represented in a quarterly publication, *The Japan Christian Quarterly*.

The largest fellowship is the post-war Evangelical Mission Association of Japan, whose position is quite similar to that of the National Association of Evangelicals in America. There are some 600 members in this association although the group actively promoting it would probably represent much less than that. The evangelical cause in Japan is promoted in their quarterly magazine, *The Japan Harvest*. Both of these magazines are given wide distribution in the churches of the missionaries' homelands, and thus have considerable influence abroad.

The third fellowship is the Japan Bible Christian Council. It was brought into existence in 1950 by missionaries who felt the need of a more forthright united evangelical witness on issues that compromise the religious freedom the state has guaranteed the church in the new constitution and against apostasy in the churches. Its purpose is to bear testimony against apostasy and idolatrous practices in the church, and to maintain fellowship among Christians who have similar convictions. Its witness has been advanced through conferences, publications, letters to the press, and a news bulletin service. *The Bible Times*, an independent quarterly magazine of one of its mission groups, also has sought to promote this witness through its Japanese and English editions.

As for the religions of Japan, Shintoism and Buddhism are still the two chief ones. General MacArthur and the Occupation Forces separated the

Japanese state from the Shinto religion, but since the end of the occupation, the "conservatives" of Japan have made an unceasing effort to restore at least recognition of some aspects of Shintoism by connecting these officially with the state and its support. The government has appointed a constitutional revision committee to recommend revision. This committee has been under the constant pressure of the Shintoists to restore Ise Shrine, the Grand Shrine of the Sun Goddess, Amaterasu Omikami, to a place of national recognition and the financial support of the national treasury. The argument has been that only Shintoism can provide the state with a national unifying force.

Some very subtle arguments have been brought forth to explain why the nation should return to Shintoism as a sort of state religion, or at least orient its patriotism to Shintoist ideology. The following quotation from Professor Y. Oishi of Kyoto University, writing on the subject of religion, the state and the constitution, reveals something of this argument:

Since the constitution was changed, the Emperor has ceased to function as the unifying factor. Instead the Diet is supposed to have replaced him as the highest authority. Therefore, if the people are permeated with a spirit of respect for the decisions of the Diet, even when they are opposed to them as individuals, the solidarity of the Japanese people will not suffer even though the emperor system has been changed. But actually there is a strong tendency not to respect the Diet's decisions when these are displeasing. This endangers the unity of the nation. Consequently, since there is no point in the present constitution which can be relied upon to provide unity, there are some people who advocate revival of the emperor system. They think that if the Diet is ineffective it may be necessary to make the Emperor the unifying factor . . . . The Occupation treated shrines as religious institutions. But I have my doubts regarding this, particularly when it comes to shrines which were built by the state as the basis of national morality . . . . The [pre-war] official view was that shrines were national institutions indicating the object of national morality.

What is the nature of the Grand Shrine of Ise which enshrines the ancestors of the Emperor? Can the state establish and maintain a shrine, dedicated to the ancestors of one who was the sovereign under the previous constitution and is a symbol of the state under the present constitution, as a state institution and designate it as the object of national morality or ancestor worship for the people? The answer depends on its relationship to our national polity . . . . In every country the national polity constitutes the boundary of religious freedom. (pp. 32-34, 37)

Here the writer is clearly saying that in every land the concept of freedom of religion is limited by that nation's understanding of its national interests. It is his belief that the national interest of Japan requires the state recognition of Shinto shrines, or at least the Grand Shrine of Ise, which enshrines the ancestors of the Emperor, in order to preserve the national morality and unity of Japan. This, of course, presents a genuine threat to the true freedom of Christianity in Japan and a genuine hazard to unrestricted missionary activity. The substitution of a Shinto shrine and veneration of the Emperor and his ancestors for the national Diet as a principle of unification for the nation would, of course, also bring an end to any hope for real democracy in Japan.

Buddhism, unlike Shintoism, has been primarily a nonpolitical religion. Buddhism receives its primary support from older people—those whose loved ones have passed on and those who realize that the years of their sojourn in this world are becoming fewer. In Japan, Buddhism has even been called the religion of the dead and dying. The greatest Buddhist festival is the annual Obon, when the souls of the dead are welcomed back and felicitated for a few days. The chief object of Buddhist worship in the home, the *butsudan*, is centered around the worship of the spirits of the deceased ancestors.

The primary task of Buddhist priests today is the conducting of funerals and officiating at rites and memorial services related to the worship of the dead. Almost all funerals in Japan are Buddhist. In more recent years, however, Buddhists have occasionally participated in protests directed toward the government. These have usually been in cases where they felt their particular interests were being discriminated against, as when they protested the placing of a large Christmas tree in front of Tokyo's national railway station as favoritism to Christianity. Another illustration was their protest to the government over President Eisenhower's proposed visit to the Shinto Meiji Shrine in 1960, the grounds being that the Shintoists had no right to such special recognition under a constitution in which all religions were to be treated equally by the state.

There are, however, some new religions with Buddhist origins that have come to considerable prominence in the postwar era and that have become very active in politics. One of these is Sokka Gakai. Sokka Gakai began in 1930 as an offspring of Nichiren Buddhism, which is a Japanese version going back over 700 years. Since the war, this ultra-rightist religious movement has had a phenomenal success, growing from 35,000 households in 1953 to over one million in 1959. "During one year, 1958, the number of new believers outnumbered the total number of Christians in Japan. The present strength is about 4,200,000 believers or, through a brief existence of 13 years, seven times more than the number of Japanese Christians. The present rate of growth is close to 100,000 persons every month" (Thomsen, p. 22).

Sokka Gakai devotees are known for their inflammatory fanaticism and activity. They are intensely politically minded, having boldly stated their intention to win the majority of the seats in both houses of Parliament within two decades and to become Japan's state religion. Their remarkable success in having their candidates elected has given Japanese politicians serious concern.

"That many of these votes were won with inflammatory fanaticism, intimidation and even threats and bribery is common knowledge—several S. G. people were sent to prison for breaking the election laws—but it must also be acknowledged that most of the votes were due to the surprisingly efficient propaganda machine of S. G. and to the fact that there are a large number of strong personalities in Sokka Gakai" (Thomsen, p. 28).

A conquest at the polls and dominance in the government by such a fanatical ultra-rightist religious organization, whose avowed goal is to be the nation's state religion, would be a true hazard for religious freedom and a great impediment to the progress of the gospel.

In any discussion of the religious state situation in Japan, the factor of communism cannot be overlooked. No group would object more strongly to being called a religion than international communism, but that their ideology has religious overtones is clear. If we were to draw out the parallel we could say that "the cause" is their god; Marx, Engels, and Lenin, their Bible; capitalism, their devil; "the right," whatever furthers their cause; heaven, their future earthly utopia; and repentance and conversion a hating of other systems and turning from them to communism. Communists may not talk in terms of religion, but they have a *summum bonum*, a worldwide conquest by communism, and dedicate their lives to it with fanatical zeal.

The communist ideology has not made its greatest progress in Japan under its own name. Communists have never had more than a few seats in the Diet as official representatives of the party. Their ideology has made its greatest progress in the Socialist Party, the labor unions (especially communication and transportation), university faculties and student bodies, writers' guilds, and the liberal church. Following the occupation's release of their leaders from Japanese prisons after the war, communists had a wonderful opportunity awaiting them. The youth of the land had no interest in the old religions of Shintoism and Buddhism, and school teachers could no longer teach the Emperor system with loyalty to Japan and love of the Emperor as the *summum bonum*. Moral, intellectual, and religious vacuums existed, giving an ideal opportunity to the communists to spread their antimilitarist, anticapitalist, socialist, and pseudo-democratic concepts.

The communist goal was to neutralize Japan's help to the free world as an Asian citadel of freedom by turning the nation into a socialist state, a utopia where everybody would own the same and where no longer would there be a few fantastically rich and the masses extremely poor, as in pre-war days. This goal won the hearts of a great many of the university students. Some 300,000 of them, in the left wing union called "Zengakuren," are dedicated to the communist ideology, though perhaps 50 percent of them are not necessarily pro-Soviet and are called by the other half "Trotskyites." Both wings of the Zengakuren, however, want to see the government of Japan overthrown, as the Russian government was overthrown in 1917. They want to see Japan become a thoroughgoing socialist state, which really means a communist one. Should this eventuate, and it is a possibility in almost any Asian country today, genuine freedom of religion would cease to exist, and the progress of the gospel would be greatly circumscribed or entirely stopped.

The Struggle for Power

These then are the primary factors involved in the state-church struggle in Japan, factors which could be closely paralleled in many other Asian or African mission lands. We need now to consider the struggle for power produced by these tensions and its relation to religious freedom. The participants are basically the old conservatives (the rightists, the Shinto nationalists, represented in Parliament by the Liberal Democratic Party), and the leftists (holding the communist ideology, represented in the Diet by the Socialist Party). Freedom of religion is at stake in the struggle between these two powers. Both of them seek to remodel the state along lines that will strengthen their position and enable them to achieve their goal. The former desires constitutional revision and the making of new laws to re-elevate Shintoism to a preferred status, as a sort of state religion, to be the basis of national unity and moral education in the schools. It also seeks the abolition of the pacifist clause in the constitution. The latter power, as long as it is a minority power, seeks to defend the present constitution and to bring about the overthrow of the government by victory at the polls or, whenever it feels it to be advantageous, by riotous measures.

Up to the present, God has, in His providence, kept each of these forces from achieving its goal by preserving a balance of power between them so that neither can get the two-thirds majority in both Houses of Parliament necessary to bring about constitutional revision. Whenever patriotism becomes involved in religion, Christians face times of testing. If a test of patriotism in Japan is again to become the individual's recognition of Shinto shrines, then its Christians will once again be in for a rugged time. Fear of this possibility is one of the reasons leading the majority of evangelical Christians in the land to vote against the liberal democrats and for the socialists. The dilemma of the true Christian in Japan today is that the nation is being torn between two opposite views, neither of which he knows in his heart recognizes the Christian concept of freedom of religion. The old conservatives cry that the people have lost confidence in the Diet as a unifying power. The nation must return to national Shinto shrines, venerating the ancestors of the Emperor, as a substitute for the Diet as a unifying factor, as well as a basis for moral education. To this the socialists shout in response that the people have lost confidence in the conservative government and in its dependence on the United States for security. The nation must go forward into national socialism and international neutralism. This dilemma of being caught between the old conservatives who seek to drag the country back to the past and the socialists who will take it into a Marxist despotism is the same problem now facing the Christian cause in many of the young republics throughout Asia and Africa. To what extent, then, is freedom of religion and the gospel involved in this struggle?

The position of the Shinto nationalists is that Shintoism can be considered to be supra-religious, having patriotism as its essence, and therefore can be used by the government under the new constitution, as under the old, to be the nation's unifying and moral force. The spokesman for this argument, Dr. Oishi, quoted earlier, has put the case in these words:

> If the state considers that Ise Shrine is for the guidance of the people in their national life from the standpoint of national morality, because it inculcates respect for the ancestors of the Emperor who is the symbol of the state, it is within its province to establish such facilities as may provide a standard of national morality.
>
> People today have no sense of national morality. Everyone thinks and does as he pleases. As a result, degeneration spreads rapidly, and it is very difficult to create a sound state and society. The shrine system in the past aimed at providing a national standard for morality apart from the personal faith of the people. Shrines were intended to strengthen the conscious recognition of the state. Therefore, when we speak from the standpoint of Japan's legal system, it is wrong to think of the shrines simply as religion, as was done by the Occupation. (pp. 38-39)
>
> +++
>
> In conclusion, although freedom of religion is recognized in the Constitution, it cannot escape control by the state when it comes into conflict with the fundamental legal order which constitutes the state, namely, Japanese national polity . . . .
>
> The fundamental reason for religious freedom being guaranteed by the Constitution lies in the fact that this is a matter which concerns the individual's inner life. However, religious freedom does not permit an unlimited expression of religion in social conduct. On the contrary, the limits of religious freedom in whatever age or country are determined by the most essential condition for an orderly society. What is the most essential condition? It is the national polity of each age and each country. (p. 90)

His contention is that, in every land, freedom of religion is necessarily limited, at least to some extent, by the national self-interest of the state. He says, "I insist that there is no sphere of human life in which the state cannot interfere when conditions are such that stability and mutual prosperity are otherwise impossible . . . . How is the area of permissible restriction to be defined? In my opinion, the national polity constitutes the key point in any consideration of limitations on the relationship between state and religion" (pp. 28, 30). He refers to the Quakers arrested in World War I for an American illustration that "under certain circumstances freedom must be subjected to restrictions." However, he does not mention that, in more recent years, freedom from military activity has been granted to conscientious objectors. For example, individuals have been excused by the Supreme Court from saluting the flag on the grounds of religious conviction, in the interests of religious freedom.

Following this principle of limitation of religious freedom when the state deems such freedom is prejudicial to the best interests of civil society, he argues that historically Japan's national polity (*kokutai*) has been based on a Shinto-Emperor relationship. The Emperor and Shinto shrines dedicated to his ancestors have been at the core, and recognition of their supreme nature serves as the basis of unification and morality. The rationale states that only this kind of national polity has worked in the past and only it will work now to keep the state from disintegration. Therefore, religious freedom must be limited so as not to interfere with this national polity nor to keep anyone from participating in it. Thus he would favor the restoration of the Grand Shrine of Ise, dedicated to the Sun Goddess as the first ancestor of the imperial line, to the position of a national Shinto shrine and the center of national morality, "because it inculcates respect for the ancestors of the Emperor who is the symbol of the state."

If a Westerner were to ask, what has bowing before a Shinto shrine got to do with improving the nation's morals, a modern Japanese Shinto nationalist would reply something like this: "It would return the people to realizing that real moral virtue, their highest good, is to live for the nation by doing the will of the Emperor, who the new constitution declares to be the symbol of the nation. The shrines dedicated to the Emperor's ancestors are the nation's tie with the past, the past generations of their forefathers and emperors, and obeisance before these shrines is expressive of their intent to continue to live for the glory of Japan by doing the will of the Emperor as their forefathers did. This not only sets the standard for what is morally good but also gives each individual the incentive of patriotism to work for it." The remark could be made of this line of reasoning, however, that, instead of preserving the Emperor as the symbol of the nation, it seems rather to make the nation the symbol of the Emperor, his will becoming its supreme guide. Historically, his will was determined for him by the oligarchy who had control of the military power.

This whole argument of trying to elevate patriotism and nationalism to the level of morals, so that religious freedom can be limited to behavior becoming the state's interpretation of patriotism, is a very clever and subtle one. It is true of course that democratic states recognizing religious freedom, which have historically been those under the influence of Christian principles, have also limited claims to freedom of religion to those areas where moral practices, in the Judeo-Christian tradition of the second table of the Ten Commandments at least, have not been disregarded. The Mormon claim to religious freedom for plural marriages was rejected by the United States government and their religious rite made unlawful on the grounds that it was immoral and undermined the social order. Where morality in the sense of improper marriage or sex relations, or molestation of persons or others' property, is not involved, religious liberty must recognize freedom of belief and practice.

For the Christian who accepts the Bible as God's special revelation, the matter of what are basically correct moral standards is already settled. He knows also that God has called upon men to render unto Him that which is His due and unto the state that which is its due. Further, he knows that he must observe the moral standards of God and worship Him obediently, and that if the state encroaches in this area, either to demand some worship for its prescribed objects or to deny some to God, he must obey God rather than man. If the state tries to include what has been known for centuries to be religious rites into its concept and standard of patriotism, if it demands that acquiescence is necessary as a demonstration of maintaining national morality, and further, that the limits of religious freedom do not extend to cover those who disregard the nation's standards of "morality," then the Christian must recognize the injustice of the demand and refuse compliance. Religious liberty demands freedom of conscience for each individual to determine when religious practice is so involved that he cannot participate. That Japanese Shintoism has the essential ingredients of pagan religion inextricably in it has already been pointed out.

Yet there are leaders in the Christian church in Japan who have recently joined the call for a recognition of Shinto shrines as only patriotic and not religious symbols. Dr. Matsushita, president of the Episcopalian St. Paul's University of Tokyo, is one who has appealed for this accommodation.

Shinto shrines are a symbol of patriotism. It is not contradictory for Buddhists and Christians to worship at Shinto shrines. I do not ignore the fact that Shinto shrine worship and patriotism are closely connected. Buddhists and Christians should not feel any contradiction in doing so, and I, as a Christian, do not. As for me, shrines are not objects of faith but symbols of my beloved country. In this meaning, it is correct to regard the Shinto shrines as being in a different category from other religions. Shinto shrines are considered usually as belonging to a religious category like Buddhism and Christianity. They must be developed along the lines of patriotic symbols. In order to enhance the sovereignty of the State, but not to the extent of deifying it, it is most desirable to have the shrines not considered religious. (p. 16)

A further quotation from missionary J. G. Vos is to the point here:

To say that the cult of the sun goddess Amaterasu Omikami has nothing to do with religion does not make it right for the Lord's people to participate in the worship of the sun goddess; it only means that the sin of dishonesty is added to that of idolatry. The pity is that so many are deceived by such palpable conceits, which must result in dreadful injury to their own consciences in the end. (p. 8)

When faith in old religions collapses for the younger generation, and Western democracy moves into a situation where there is no foundation of Christian standards or morality, chaos can ensue. This is what has happened in Japan to a certain extent. Juvenile delinquency has skyrocketed until the majority of arrests are among teenagers. "Everyone thinks and does as he pleases," or at least it seems so at times. The former goals of living for the glory of the nation through doing the will of the Emperor as the highest morality are gone. A moral vacuum has followed in which nothing higher than self-seeking is left. But for intelligent men, least of all a church leader and educator, to advocate returning to feudal concepts to solve the problem is ridiculous obscurantism. Shinto shrine obeisance in modern Japan, as a factor for the development of patriotism and morality, will be utterly futile without the constraint of deep fear. This restraint can only be effected by a return to police state methods, and the police state would mean not only the loss of freedom of religion, but of speech as well—a forfeiture of all the freedoms now enjoyed under the new constitution. The tragedy of modern Japan is that it finds itself in this moral dilemma and has no real solution within itself to which to turn. This but points at the urgency of the need for the Christian gospel and God's revealed standards for this nation and all nations of the world. If the nation turns to "the road back" to solve the moral problem then the church can once again expect to be subjected to great pressure to allow its covenant children to bow before the Shinto shrines. Persecution and dictatorship will inevitably follow.

If the socialists are the eventual victors in the present power struggle, on the other hand, what can be expected? The Socialist Party in Japan is so dominated by communists and communist ideology that its control of the state can certainly be expected to result in great limitations of freedom of religion and speech, as in every other country where the Marxist ideology has become the guiding principle. The ensuing regimentation will assuredly extend to the church and missions. The door will be opened to a flood of foreign communist experts and to a real communist takeover of the government. The church, in its largest organizations, will cooperate to a great extent through its leaders, as it is already openly sympathetic to the socialist cause and ideology. As in China, many of its leaders can be expected to be in the forefront hailing the takeover and offering to surrender many of its freedoms. An eyewitness from China has written, "The communists have set up a puppet church of compromised Christians who have often helped in the liquidation of their brethren. These 'reformed' Christians will say what the government wants them to say and act the way the government wants them to act. They have the form of godliness but have denied the power thereof" (H. H. Martinson, *Red Dragon Over China*, p. 159). The eventual reward of many of them was that they were included among the 200,000 Christians executed by the communists.

A widely read columnist in the world's largest newspaper, Japan's *Asahi Shimbun*, pointed out the Socialist Party's close relation to China's communists following their leader's visit to Peking. "In fact it really appears that the Socialist Party now no longer draws a line between itself and the Chinese communists. But while it draws no line between itself and communist China, it draws a line between itself and the Japanese Communist Party. Is this artful dodging really possible? It is indeed an odd party . . . [as] described by Mao Tsetung" (Jan. 19, 1962).

A surrender to Japanese socialism will almost inevitably be followed by a communist takeover. What will follow for those who want to live in freedom is already illustrated on the great continent of China. The genocide of the Jews under the Nazi Eichmann and the slaughter of the bourgeois farmers under Stalin were but partial demonstrations of the inhuman bestiality to which modern, natural man can descend when all moral restraint is cast off for a wicked cause in the name of a nation's good. It took Red China, however, under the demonic spirit of ruthless communism, through its malevolent executions of over 50 million common people, to show on what a vast scale brutalized man can be insensible to human suffering and hold the life of his fellow man cheaper than dirt (see Martinson, op. cit. p. 158). To think that conquest for the socialists would not soon lead to the same kind of communism in Japan as we have seen in action in China during the past decade is to be but naive dreamers like those who thought of the Chinese communists as but agrarian reformers prior to their continental victory.

The Solution

What then should be the attitude of the church as it faces such a political power struggle in the outcome of which its freedom is so deeply at stake? There are those who say that the church as institute "should stay out of politics," since the church and state are separate, and interpret this phrase to mean that the church as institute cannot bear direct witness to the government. There are some sections of the *Westminster Confession of Faith* that are worth quoting on this matter. These Reformed fathers, speaking at a critical time in the relations of church and state in 1698, yet speaking from the Word of God, declared:

God alone is lord of the conscience, and hath left it free from the doctrines and commandments of men, which are in any thing contrary to His Word, or beside it, in matters of faith or worship. So that, to believe such doctrines, or to obey such commands, out of conscience, is to betray true liberty of conscience .... God, the supreme Lord and King of all the world, hath ordained civil magistrates, to be, under Him, over the people, for His own glory, and the public good; and, to this end, hath armed them with the power of the sword, for the defence and encouragement of them that are good, and for the punishment of evildoers ... so, for that end, they may lawfully now under the

New Testament, wage war, upon just and necessary occasion . . . . [as nursing fathers, it is the duty of civil magistrates to protect the Church of our common Lord, without giving the preference to any denomination of Christians above the rest, in such a manner that all ecclesiastical persons whatever shall enjoy the full, free and unquestioned liberty of discharging every part of their sacred functions, without violence or danger] . . . . Synods and councils are to handle, or conclude, nothing, but that which is ecclesiastical: and are not to intermeddle with civil affairs which concern the commonwealth; unless by way of humble petition in cases extraordinary; or by way of advice for satisfaction of conscience, if they be thereunto required by the civil magistrate. (Chapter 20:2, 23:1-3, 31:5; bracket text contained in American revision only)

These sober, carefully enunciated principles need to be heard again today. The Church is not of the world but in the world and has a responsibility to witness for truth to its utmost. A witness to the state on fundamental matters of freedom or morality does not necessarily involve the Church "in politics." That phrase is usually construed to mean a choosing of sides between political parties and active participation on the part of one of them. Addressing a communication to the government, or to a government committee, soberly presenting the Church's position on a fundamental principle concerning freedom or morality may bring the displeasure of the state, or arouse the ire of the public. These reasons alone, however, are not adequate grounds for the Church maintaining silence. The Church may have to bear witness to the state either by way of petition or protest if its freedom to proclaim the gospel is not to be lost by forfeit. When Paul's rights as a free citizen were being infringed and his very opportunity to carry on his gospel ministry jeopardized, he did not hesitate to appeal to the state for a fair application of its law to him (Acts 21:39; 22:25; 25:10-11).

For its covenant children, the Church must make every effort to preserve religious freedom, both of worship and from state compulsion to participate in pagan practices. In the new postwar republics, clauses guaranteeing freedom of religion are not uncommon in the new constitutions, but in most of these lands, there is no tradition of freedom of religion, much less a tradition of defending and preserving it. A missionary to Africa has written an interesting comment about that dark continent:

Probably one of the outstanding characteristics of Africa today is this growing, and sometimes almost complete, disregard for the basic principles of the moral law by individual and national alike. It is true that some of the new nations have fairly good written constitutions, patterned often after some of those of the West, but by and large the written law, though embodying many of the principles of the moral law, is almost completely ignored . . . . The root of the political and economic problem of Africa is spiritual. The reason for present trends lies in SIN. The instability of present governments, the graft and corruption, the militant nationalism, the onslaught of communism is a result of disregard for the law of God. Even the poverty that stalks the land is brought on in large measure by lack of respect for the absolute law of God. Coveting the wealth of the foreigner in her midst, failing to understand (because the foreigner has not understood himself or, if he has, he has not taught it to the African) the sources of that prosperity, Africa has coveted it and sought to use the arm of force to gain it. In the process, she has destroyed the very source of economic advance, capital saved and used to increase production. In her desperation she has turned to the glowing promises which the communists are free to make but utterly unable to fulfill. In her confusion she has turned to a variety of false religions. (*Torch and Trumpet*, Jan. 1962, p. 20)

By the common grace of God, the concept of religious freedom is becoming well-known throughout the free world today, yet its real significance and legitimate methods of securing its continuance are little understood. If the church in these lands is not to see this gift of God lost by default, it may have to take the initiative in speaking out to the government, or to the public through resolutions in the newspapers, pointing out where contemplated action endangers the principle of religious freedom or overthrows it completely. Such statements of advice, or petition or protest when needed, are not only in the interest of preserving freedom for the spread of the Christian gospel for the day in which they are made, but are essential to preserve gospel freedom for the church's covenant children, and for future generations that they may hear the unadulterated gospel (Matt. 19:14; Acts 2:39).

The church is a part of a nation's society and can demonstrate its indigenous nature and sense of responsibility to society by speaking out for freedom and for its preservation and correct understanding for the benefit of all. This is especially true when constitutional guarantees of religious liberty are in jeopardy. At such a time, if other voices are not adequate in their defense of freedom, speaking out is not merely an option for the church but its solemn duty. The principle of interpretation, which declares "where a duty is commanded, the contrary sin is forbidden; and, where a sin is forbidden, the contrary duty is commanded" (*Westminster Larger Catechism*, Q. 99:4) would seem to necessitate the duty of making every effort to insure freedom of the gospel for the church's covenant children and future generations a corollary of the following words of Christ: "And whoso shall receive one such little child in my name receiveth me. But whoso shall offend one of these little ones which believe in me, it were better for him that a millstone were hanged about his neck, and that he were drowned in the depth of the sea" (Matt. 18:5-6. See also Rom. 15:1-2; Eph. 6:19-20; Ezek. 33:6; 1 Cor. 14:8).

Should the church as an organism, that is as individual Christians, also bear direct witness to the government? The individual Christian as a citizen of the state has a responsibility to work for good government, using his influence where he can. But should he also speak to the state as an individual when he believes religious freedom is threatened? "Where no counsel is, the people fall: but in the multitude of counsellors there is safety," the Scripture declares (Prov. 11:14). On the whole it would seem wise for the Christian to make his witness on such matters with other Christians or through his church and, thus, better safeguard himself, and the cause he represents, from misrepresentation. If the church refuses to bear its witness, however, and in the honest judgment of the individual Christian the reason stems from an improper understanding of its duty or from fear of the consequences, he must make the decision himself whether or not he will carry the testimony he feels necessary to the state. In addition to this, however, there are times when the individual Christian must give his witness by saying "No!" to the state (Acts 4:19-20). As a citizen, he is certainly free to work with non-Christians in a citizens' league for freedom, but he must make it clear that he speaks as a citizen and not for the church. The work of the church may not be engaged in by unbelievers, or the church work in an organizational way with unbelievers (2 Cor. 6:14-16; compare 2 Chr. 18:3 with 19:2).

What should be the role of the foreign missionary, as a Christian living in a foreign land, in a witness to the state on behalf of freedom of religion? Should he participate in the struggle to preserve religious liberty? It would certainly seem to be in the best interest of his cause to let the national Christian church deal with the government in such matters if for no other reason than to avoid any stigma that may exist toward his own country being attached to the cause he advocates. In spite of this circumstance, however, and the fact that he in a sense is a guest in a foreign land, if the church is too weak or fearful of speaking, the missionary must remember that he is, first of all, an ambassador of Christ, and must speak for his Lord. Because the new democracies emerging from previously authoritarian governments usually have no tradition or example of resisting encroachments on freedom, the missionary may first have to supply the example of how it should be done if the national church is to learn. The responsibility of leading national pastors and Christian leaders into an understanding of this ministry to the state is surely an important one.

But what means can the church use in its efforts to preserve religious freedom? Certainly not by inciting revolt against the state, for this is not the church's function (John 18:36). Nor can the church, by participating as institute, unite with citizens' leagues comprised of non-Christians to oppose the government. The task of the church is the ministry of the Word, to bring its requirements and their application to the attention of the people. The church, thus, has the right, and, in some cases, the duty, to present oral or written petitions to the state on a pertinent issue of religious freedom, to petition against some adverse action, or to protest against a *fait accompli* that compromises the principle of religious liberty.

There are also times when the church must refuse compliance to the state's edicts. In writing of the pre-war reaction of Christians and missionaries under Japanese rule in the Far East to the state's imposed Religious Bodies Law, J. G. Vos has said:

> It is very commonly stated that if the magistrate positively forbids the preaching of the gospel, then Christians ought to obey God and disobey the magistrate, but that as long as the magistrate merely proposes to license and control the preaching of the gospel, Christians ought to comply with the demand . . . . For the civil magistrate to control religion is an infringement of the people's religious liberty and a usurpation of Christ's headship over the church. All the weak and doubtful arguments that are adduced to prove

the contrary propositions fail miserably to do so, and leave the inescapable impression that they proceed not from principle but from a desire to avert untoward consequences . . . . Confronted with such demands to render the things of God to Caesar, the great majority of missionaries and Oriental Christian leaders as already stated, favor compliance. This seems to us to reveal a very serious situation and to manifest some symptoms of a very dangerous spiritual malady. (p. 16-18)

Vos gives five objections against the attitude of compliance. First, compliance proceeds from unsound ethical principles—"to do good that evil may come." Second, it proceeds from false and narrow views of the message and task of missions, interpreting the missionary task to be the preaching of the message of salvation only instead of the proclamation of the whole counsel of God. Third, it harbors the germ of a nontheistic view of life, considering the salvation of men to be the *summum bonum*, rather than the glory of God. Fourth, it proceeds from unbelief in the power of God to carry out His work in the world and to protect the Church against the assaults of all her enemies. "It is no part of our duty to keep the door open for preaching the gospel by compromising with moral evil." Fifth, compliance even from the viewpoint of the pragmatic test of results is certain ultimately to fail to accomplish that which is expected of it by its advocates. Appeasement fails, for it proves but to be the first of a series of steps down the slippery pathway to complete capitulation to the demands of the state. "When once it becomes evident that the spirit of compromise has infected the forces of Christianity, the thirst of the totalitarian state for complete domination over Christian institutions becomes unquenchable" (Vos, p. 18-20).

In cases where Christian churches find themselves suddenly confronted by the state's abandonment of the principle of freedom of religion, they have only two courses of action. Either they can compromise and comply with the state's demands, as did most denominations under the Japanese Religious Bodies Law, or they can offer noncompliance. The Christian course certainly seems to be to follow the example of the early Christians to pray for holy boldness with which to stand fast for the faith (Acts 4:19-20, 23-31). They can well heed the proverb, "It's better to hang together than to hang separately," and join with those of like precious faith in united evangelical action to seek freedom for the church's faith and life. In our day the greatest threat to the freedom of the church in Asia and Africa is the possibility of a communist conquest of the state. The history of such events indicates clearly that the communist aim for the church includes both the goal of the complete domination of the church and the reaching of this objective by gradual and subtle steps. The Christian should know that this is the case and expect it. The possibility of the church going underground, as did the Christians of the catacomb days, in this age of rapid transportation, instant communication, and extensive population seems to be unrealistic. The possibility, also, of making small compromises with the demands of the communist state in the hope of escaping more serious demands for compromise is even more unrealistic, as is also the hope of a Christian going unnoticed and being faced with no demands that would compromise his Christian principles. There seems to be little alternative for a true Christian than to follow the teaching of Peter, or the example of the Christian hero in Peking, Wang Ming Tao, who refused to compromise Christian truth or discontinue group worship and was ready to suffer the consequence. The Word of God is explicit on this in a day when the apostles faced a similar situation:

> But and if ye suffer for righteousness' sake, happy are ye: and be not afraid of their terror, neither be troubled; but sanctify the Lord God in your hearts; and be ready always to give an answer to every man that asketh you a reason of the hope that is in you with meekness and fear: Having a good conscience; that, whereas they speak evil of you, as of evildoers, they may be ashamed that falsely accuse your good conversation in Christ. For it is better, if the will of God be so, that ye suffer for well doing, than for evil doing . . . . Beloved, think it not strange concerning the fiery trial which is to try you, as though some strange thing happened unto you: But rejoice, inasmuch as ye are partakers of Christ's sufferings; that, when his glory shall be revealed, ye may be glad also with exceeding joy. (1 Pet. 3:14-17; 4:12-13)

When an evil, absolutistic regime seizes the government, the Christian and his church might as well make up their minds that if it is God's will to let evil come to such power, escape is well nigh impossible. It may be God's will to intervene on the part of some individuals to remove them from this terrible plight, but the Christian must be ready to do as Peter describes, that is, to "suffer for righteousness' sake." He must faithfully refuse compliance with the state's demands which compromise Christian principles (Acts 4:19-20).

God has ordained that the Christian "should render unto Caesar the things that are Caesar's, and unto God the things that are God's." God has also ordained that the state's civil magistrate "is the minister of God to thee for good." If the state actively violates this duty, the Christian can only manfully declare his position to the authorities and be ready to pay the price, leaving the outcome in the hands of God who has said, "Vengeance is mine; I will repay, saith the Lord."

Questions for Study and Discussion

1. From where does the state derive its authority?
2. Define "religious freedom."
3. How was the relationship between religion and state characterized in pre-war Japan?
4. Compare the reactions of the church in Japan to governmental demands that it give obeisance to the Emperor with the reaction of the church in the early Roman Empire to similar demands.
5. What part do the following "isms" play in the life of Japan today: Shinto-ism, Buddhism, Sakka Gakkaiism, communism, socialism?
6. What is the chief political dilemma the Christian faces in Japan today?
7. What is the moral dilemma faced by Japan today?
8. What is the scriptural relationship of the church to the state? The individual Christian to the government? The missionary to the government?
9. How can the church best work toward the preservation of religious freedom?

Part 3:
The Destination

8

The Church's Mission to the Nations

"It should give pause to timid souls, who fearfully insist year after year that their home church must first be established thoroughly before a foreign missionary effort can be launched, to realize what God required of the Antioch church after just one year."

T he reference to the nations here is primarily to the peoples of those lands where the gospel of Christ is unknown or little known—the countries of Asia, Africa, and South America where the true Word of God has been but little proclaimed. The nations of North America and Europe do not need it any less, but their real need is to listen to and believe the gospel upon which their great churches were founded. This need is written in the Bibles on their bookshelves and is literally being cried to them from the housetops through their radio and T.V. antenna.

There are vast masses of people in eastern and southern nations today of whom it can truly be said that gross darkness covers the people. These are the nations who either have heard nothing, or else heard so remotely that they have no realization of its significance, of the fact that, in these last days, God has revealed Himself from heaven and sent His Son to earth with marvelous light for their dark existences. These are the people who live in daily fear and face the solemn tomorrow of death with dark dread. They do not know of the eternal truths of God and so live for self, governed by expediency, seeking gain where they can, ready for any compromise of truth for survival, trying to satisfy their God-given religious sense with the dregs of polytheistic superstition.

To these nations, the Church of Christ has a great mission. Indeed, in this mission, the Church reveals that its very essence for the primary mark of a true church is its faithful preaching of the Word of God. It is a serious misconception to think of this requirement being met by the mere preaching of the Word over and over again to the same group of believers, for Christ's commission to His Church was that through them by the empowering of His Holy Spirit, the gospel must be preached to the whole world. The Church's mission to the nations is thus the work of the Triune God through His Church of sending Christ's ambassadors to all nations to proclaim His whole Word for the salvation of lost men, the establishing of churches, and the expansion of His kingdom, all for the glory of God, according to His eternal purpose. Now let us undertake a consideration of this mission of the Church to the nations, first as to its basis, and then as to its objective.

God's Eternal Purpose

For those who believe in the final authority of biblical revelation, the ultimate ground of the Church's mission to the nations must be the Triune God's eternal purpose as revealed in the Scriptures. Ephesians 3:1-11 clearly confirms this. The passage is a forceful presentation of God's eternal purpose that His Church should take His gospel to all the Gentile nations. In verse four, Paul is speaking of the mystery of Christ that was not known in Old Testament times as it is now revealed. It is that the Gentiles are to be made fellow members of the body of Christ. Paul himself says he was called to preach the gospel to them. This ministry will make all see what is God's plan or dispensation; which is not that the proclamation of the gospel will be carried out by angels but rather, in a sense, for the angels, too, that they may see the many-sided wisdom of God in doing it through men, redeemed men, His Church. We might well expect that Christ, having laid down His life in the cause of man's redemption, would want to commit the proclamation of the message—which cost Him so dearly—to the most reliable messengers, the sinless angels. But it is not to be so! We who have been made fellow members in His Church are to take His message to the nations. Christ accomplished the redemption, but His Church is to proclaim its message. This is God's eternal purpose.

The unveiling of this mystery does not imply that God is revealing a sudden and new interest in the Gentile nations. On the contrary, Paul, as he preached to the Gentiles, emphasized that God had never left Himself without a witness to them, but had continuously revealed His goodness through the dispensation of His common grace through natural blessings. He has long suffered their wicked ways and endured their idolatry, but now desires to send them personal ambassadors through His Church, to tell them of His love, and to command them to repent of their rebellion against Him. God's plan calls for the Church's sending out of His message of pardon through Christ, to all who will believe, throughout all the domains of Satan. That usurper prince and god of this world, the deceiver who stole the affections of men from God, must be exposed, and men called upon to repent of the ways of his kingdom of darkness and to turn to God's kingdom of light. This is God's plan and purpose of the ages.

When our Lord came to inaugurate the New Covenant age, God's plan that the divine message of salvation should be given a proclamation to every nation began to come into focus. From the very beginning of His ministry, Christ evidenced a deep concern that the message of His benevolent kingdom should be given an ever wider presentation. Luke records that as Jesus set out to preach He declared, "I must preach the kingdom of God to other cities also; for therefore am I sent" (Luke 4:43). Later He declared that the fulfillment of His purpose for a universal proclamation of the gospel was a necessary preliminary to His return to earth to end this age. "And this gospel of the kingdom shall be preached in all the world for a witness unto all nations; and then shall the end come" (Matt. 24:14).

If Christ's disciples realized the real significance of this pronouncement—that the worldwide proclamation was to be done by human effort, by Christ's disciples—they must have been inwardly amazed. How could it be done? They were but the commonest of people, living in a small, enemy-occupied land under a military dictatorship. When and how could Christ's message ever escape from its bounds and reach to all the nations? If they were to be hated by the nations, afflicted and killed, did not this insure its failure? How then could it be done? The answer was soon to come.

On the occasion of His last appearance before His apostles on earth, our Lord laid down to these first officers of His Church a great imperative that spelled out the Church's mission to the nations for all time. "All power is given unto me in heaven and earth. Go ye therefore and teach all nations" (Matt. 28:18-19). The mission could succeed because Christ possessed authority and power to launch it and bring it to completion. The commission of the Church's first officers, and of all their successors, to a worldwide task was grounded in the commission of the Son by the Father. The Father had given Him all authority to provide for the proclamation of His message to all nations and to build His Church. The risen Son, in the name of this authority by which He had been sent and with which He had been invested, was the Commissioner. "As my Father hath sent me, even so send I you" (John 20:21). "All authority is given unto me . . . . Go therefore and make disciples!"

This Great Commission is the complement of the Great Confession. It was the provision for the continuation of the Apostle's Great Confession and the fulfillment of Christ's Great Declaration that followed it. Peter had confessed, "Thou art the Christ, the Son of the living God," and Christ had declared, "Upon this rock I will build my church: and the gates of hell shall not prevail against it. And I will give unto thee the keys of the kingdom of heaven" (Matt. 16:16-19). How was He then to build His Church? By His sent-ones going forth with the confession of Peter to all nations to make disciples. The Church, through its officers, with the authority of Christ, is to provide for the spread of the confessional message by which and on which the expanding Church is to be built. It is to do so by taking that message to all the nations.

The Church is to propagate the Church. Its mission is to reproduce itself, to multiply through its individual members witnessing the redemptive message of Christ to their neighbors, through its corporate witness to the community, and through its missionaries sent forth to the uttermost parts with the good news that Jesus is the Son of God who will save all who come unto Him in faith. This is the eternal purpose of God, that the Gentiles should be made fellow members of the one body of Christ, by the preaching of the gospel to the nations, not by the angels but by the Church (Eph. 3:10), that both men and angels should see the manifold wisdom of God in planning it this way.

The Acts' data well demonstrate how clearly the apostles understood this to be God's plan of the ages for the building of His Church and their supreme task. A key is the symbol of responsibility and authority, and Peter went forward with those given him to unlock the gate of admittance to Christian life and service to the Jews at Pentecost, and to the Gentiles in the home of Cornelius. The Acts narrative then tells how Paul took the keys given him to Antioch, at the call of Barnabas, and how together they labored there for one year. It should give pause to timid souls, who fearfully insist year after year that their home church must first be established thoroughly before a foreign missionary effort can be launched, to realize what God required of the Antioch church after just one year. The Holy Spirit ordered its officers to take its two most able preachers and send them out as missionaries. The church did not hesitate but commissioned them to go forth on their mission to the nations. They returned to report how the Lord had opened the gates of heaven to many through their ministry, and the church sent them out again "to be a light of the Gentiles . . . for salvation unto the ends of the earth" (Acts 13:47). Souls were saved; believers baptized in the triune Name; churches organized and elders ordained to govern and teach.

Again they returned to report and again the church sent them out. This time, however, an altercation arose that might seem to stop the church's outreach. It furnished evidence, however, that God would not allow anything to overthrow His eternal purpose of reaching all the nations with His message from heaven. The Lord demonstrated that, even though we have the treasure of His Word in the earthen vessels of fallible flesh, He would make the wrath of man to praise Him in order to provide for the forward progress of His message. The dispute that broke up the gospel team of Paul and Barnabas resulted in two teams going forth and thus doubling the area reached. It was but the beginning of many illustrations down through church history of how God would overrule the tragic differences and frailties of men and cause them in one way or another to contribute to the spread of His Word. To recognize this, however, is neither to justify the differences nor lessen the need of a reconciliation. Thank God Paul could later say of Mark "he is profitable to me for the ministry" (2 Tim. 4:11).

The driving inner compulsion of the love of God and concern for lost men drove Paul ever forward on the Church's mission to the nations. "A great necessity is laid upon me," he wrote the Corinthian church. "Woe is unto me, if I preach not the gospel!" (1 Cor. 9:16) From there he wrote to Rome and told of his desire to preach there also and then to go on into Spain. "How shall they hear without a preacher?" he asked. "And how shall they preach, except they be sent?" (Rom. 10:14-15) Later, in prison again for the gospel's sake, he wrote to his young protégé Timothy, "I endure all things for the elect's sakes, that they may also obtain the salvation of Christ" (2 Tim. 2:10). Here is concern, compassion for the lost, the mood of a man whose heart is in tune with the heart of Christ. Is such concern ours for the lost whose tragic condition moved our Lord with compassion? How deeply are we motivated by the love of God to aim at making His name glorious throughout the world, and to bring men into His kingdom from every nation, that there might be some to do His will in all the earth? The task of taking His message of love and redemption to every creature is the task He has left us to do.

The Scripture, then, makes crystal clear that the basis of the Church's mission to the nations rests in God's eternal purpose that all nations shall have the message of His pardon to those who receive His Son, proclaimed to them by the efforts not of His angels but of His Church, moved by His love and aiming at His glory to the end that some shall enter His kingdom "out of every kindred, and tongue, and people, and nation" (Rev. 5:9).

Scriptural Authority

A commitment to the Bible as the infallibly inspired Word of God, the Church's final authority in its missionary enterprise, lays a firm basis for the Church's mission to the nations, as earlier noted, but one that also makes the objectives of that mission clear. Since in contemporary theology this biblical authority is widely rejected, however, it is well first to note the confusion in mission theology and objective that this rejection produces. The year 1961 was a very significant one in the history of world missions. In November, an event of significance took place in New Delhi, India, when the International Missionary Council, liaison and representative organ of most of the older and larger mission boards of the ecumenical denominations, merged with the organization of the World Council of Churches.

In anticipation of this event, and the need of endeavoring to unify their thinking on the theology and objectives of the Church's mission, leaders of the ecumenical movement gave considerable consideration to this matter. The publication of the book *The Theology of the Christian Mission*, a comprehensive symposium of essays by such well-known contemporary scholars as Barth, Cullman, Kraemer, F. H. Ross, Benz, Tillich, and many others, reflects this concern and presents the latest conclusions of the writing theologians. The majority of them provide a startling revelation of how far the rejection of the finality of biblical authority has progressed, preparing the way for an acceptance of pagan religions as a foundation on which to build a Christian structure. A few illustrations will suffice.

Professor Paul Tillich of Harvard University, for instance, supports the concept of the continuity of all religions and of Christianity as their fulfillment. Writing on the subject "Missions and History," he declares, "People are not outside of God; they are grasped by God on the level in which they can be grasped in their experience of the Divine, in the realm of holiness in which they are living . . . even though the symbols in which the Holy is expressed may seem extremely primitive and idolatrous" (p. 286-287). Again he states, "First of all, one should not misunderstand missions as an attempt to save from eternal damnation as many individuals as possible among the nations of the world" (p. 283). According to Tillich, the task of missions is not "the attempt to save individual souls . . . . Rather, it is the attempt to transform the latent Church—which is present in the world religions, in paganism, Judaism and humanism—into something new: the New Reality in Jesus as the Christ" (p. 284). Thus for Tillich, the Church being conceived of as "latently present" in the pagan religions, the objective of the Church's mission is not that of seeking to convert from heathen religions but of bringing that which is latent in them into existential experience.

Professor A. C. Bouquet of Andhra University in India, writing on the theme "Revelation and the Divine Logos," advances the thesis that John's use of the term *logos* indicates his adoption of the Hellenistic thought forms of Jews and Greeks. This he believes was a Holy Spirit-directed effort to relate "the Christian God-story to the religious beliefs of the Gentile world" (p. 184). He emphasizes that "some sort of incarnation of the Cosmic Logos, albeit usually a mythical one, was a familiar idea to many educated Gentiles at the time when the Johannine writings came to be composed . . . ." (p. 187). "Whether they accept Christ or not," he declared, those who seek to interpret the universe by "a single supreme formula, moral and spiritual as well as physical" reveal that "they are certainly living *kata logon* [according to the Logos]" (p. 194). Thus it is possible to think, he says, of "Christian Buddhists, Christian Moslems, Christian Vedantists and Christian Confucians and Taoists." (p. 198).

Professor Floyd H. Ross of Southern California's School of Theology, writing on "The Christian Mission in Larger Dimension" dogmatically asserts,

> All of the early Christians' affirmations about Jesus the Christ were in the mythic dimension. They believed that Christ was in some sense the "Messiah," or the "Son of Man," or the "Son of God." Some believed that he had a "virgin birth." All of these themes are ancient mythic themes, paralleled over and over again in the religions of mankind. That God "chose" one race to be "his people," that Jesus was a preexistent "divine being" whose coming marks the end of the "present age," that God let "His Son" die on a cross in order that the "Son's" death might obtain "atonement for the sins of man,". . . that "there is no other name under heaven given among men by which we must be saved"—all of this is mythic. (p. 221-222)

For Ross, "The Christian mission today involves bearing witness to a profound search for living truth which can never be confined within any language, theological or non-theological, Christian or non-Christian" (p. 214). With Ross, the Christian message and mission have become completely subjective and relative.

Professor Ernest Benz of Marbury University has the theme, "Ideas for a Theology of the History of Religion." He rejects the antithesis between the Christian and the pagan heart and declares of

> those who have never heard of him [Jesus], heathen and non-Christians, who to their own surprise turn out to be Christians because they have fulfilled the command of love, will be received into the Kingdom of God . . . . The criterion which determines the consignment of men into the Kingdom of God or to outer darkness is not a definite doctrine about Christ, not a recognition of the Christian claim to absoluteness, nor is it even a knowledge of the historical figure of Jesus. (p. 143-144)

One who is himself the product of this type of mission theology, Professor Masatohi Doi of Japan's Doshisha University School of Theology, contributes his views in an essay on "The Nature of Encounter between Christianity and Other Religions as Witnessed on the Japanese Scene." He reflects the underlying Buddhist philosophy, so close to the surface in much of Japanese theology. "No historical event," he declares, "can be ultimately meaningful unless there is an experiencing subject who accepts it as ultimately meaningful. And no experiencing subject can produce the ultimately meaningful event" (p. 175). For him, "Christianity as an historical religion is a distorted response to the divine act and as such stands under the judgment of God just as do all other religions" (p. 173). Sixty years of modernist missions in Japan have produced a strain of contemporary theologians there whose virulent attack on historic Christianity outdoes that of even their teachers.

The transcendental theologians, such as Barth and Kraemer, strive to build their theology of missions and objectives from an interpretation of a Bible held to be wholly fallible yet nonetheless the instrument through which the revelation of God comes to man. On the whole, there appears to be a genuine reluctance to consider the objective of missions in terms of seeking to save men from hell, the just reward for their sin, and such a presentation is missing. The testimony of Scripture is not brought out on this matter in spite of the place given the Bible as containing man's witness to the revelation of God.

Erroneous Theology

The confused and confusing views of these contemporary theologians, who try to lay a basis for the Church's mission to the nations without recourse to the Scriptures as the final authority, yet a basis from which they expect to derive the proper objectives of the missionary enterprise, leave one wondering if on such a basis the Church has a legitimate mission at all. Their view of the Gentile world in its religious manifestations is a far cry from that of Paul in the opening chapter of his epistle to the Romans. To Paul, and other biblical writers, the need of a mission to the Gentile nations was based on the present nature of man and the nature of his unbelief. Man, Scripture makes clear, although created in the image of God as an upright creature and innocent of sin, following his expulsion from paradise as a morally and spiritually fallen being in rebellion against the Creator, is unable and unwilling to do anything to please God, although still retaining the image attributes of a rational, moral, and religious creature.

It is of the nature of unbelief of the natural man, pagan in his heart as he is, to repress the God-consciousness with which he was created and its response to the revelation of God in nature. Although God, as Paul testified to the heathen Gentile nations, was no foreigner to their skies in that His eternal power and deity were revealed there, and His benevolence was revealed in the sun and the rain He sent to them to make bountiful their crops and do them good, yet today they still repress or distort all this testimony. The heathen try to placate the inner, God-given desire to worship by substituting creature worship, "worshiped and served the creature more than the Creator" (Rom. 1:25), wherefore they are under God's condemnation and are without excuse. But now, Paul declares in his sermon to the Gentiles, God is willing to overlook all this past rebellion and idolatry, if they will repent of it, renounce the ways of the kingdom of the usurper god of this world, and will believe on God's Son from heaven for the salvation of their souls and entrance into His kingdom of light. Paul's theology, in contrast to that of the would-be framers of the theology of the Christian mission, gives a firm basis for a mission to the Gentiles, and also sets the course for its objectives.

An erroneous theology of missions can only produce an erroneous missionary objective. If Christian truth is latent in pagan religion, if there is a continuity between the beliefs of heathen worship and Christian faith so that Christianity is but the fulfillment of the ancient non-Christian religions, then the objective of converting from these religions to Christianity vanishes. Rather, the objective becomes one of trying to get the heathen to realize that which is latent in their religions and to live in fuller conformity to it, and thus become "Christian" Buddhists, or "Christian" Hindus, or perhaps even "Christian" animists! The missionary endeavor that follows this line of theological thought cannot but lose its real significance as a Christian mission. The post-war woman, educational missionary of the United Church of Canada, who is quoted in an article entitled "New Model Missionary" in a May 1961 Canadian magazine, is an illustration of this when she says, "In the past we used to believe that we came to bring Christ to Africa. Now we know that we come to find Christ here" (*The Cape Breton Post*, p. 31).

The problem of the contemporary mission theology of the ecumenical movement seems to be that a large segment of its writers have completely confused special and general revelation. They have reduced what we know to be God's special revelation, the Holy Scriptures, to a fallible record where witness to revelation may be found, and declared general revelation adequate to enable the heathen to enter the kingdom of God. Thus Benz can write, "Paul emphasizes here the continuity of the self-witness of the living God throughout the whole series of human generations. . . . It is completely off the track here to speak of an absolute discontinuity between Christianity and the history of religion before Christianity. . . . Jesus promises that even those who have never heard of him, heathen and non-Christians . . . will be received into the Kingdom of God" (p. 142-144).

There is indeed a continuity of God's witness throughout the ages in that He made man in His own image with an ineradicable God-consciousness, and by His common grace and general revelation has never left Himself without a witness in nature to all men everywhere. But we cannot derive from this the modern theology of the continuity of non-Christian religious beliefs and Christian truth, for there is also the continuity of the response of natural man to the witness of God to which Paul refers. It is the continuity of response of repressing his inner God-consciousness and giving a distorted interpretation to the significance of the created universe, of general revelation, indicated by his turning to creature worship and rejecting the Creator. Without the light of special revelation to bring fallen man a knowledge of God's provision for his forgiveness and redemption through Jesus Christ, and the regenerating power of His Holy Spirit to enable him to accept it by faith, there can be no entrance into the kingdom of God.

The goal of a mission enterprise oriented to this erroneous theology of the modern ecumenical movement is no longer that of seeking to build a Christian Church and society through the conversion of individuals, but that of trying to build a new society by stimulating the assumed latent spiritual good in the natural man and his religion, and directing this towards the forwarding of a program of social reform. Dr. R. B. Manikan, frequent spokesman for the International Missionary Council, has elucidated this objective of contemporary missions in an address to Union Seminary students entitled "A New Era in the World Mission of the Church." He states:

> In the new era of Missions, not only our missionary vocabulary but also our theology and our outlook should change. . . . We need to present the whole Gospel to the whole man. . . . It is no longer sufficient to open colleges, hos-

pitals and orphanages to attract non-Christians to the Church. While you are caring for their bodies and cultivating their minds, social forces are working against you. No, the preaching of the Gospel must be accompanied by the proclamation of social and economic justice. (p. 36)

But why do we need to change our theology and outlook, we may ask, to present the whole gospel to the whole man? If we preach the gospel for the conversion of fallen man and the whole Word of God to make them faithful disciples, are we not laying the true basis for a just society? On the other hand, can such a basis be laid until the Holy Spirit has wrought the new life in men through the gospel we bring? The only alternative to a Church conceiving its mission to the nations being a crusade for social and economic justice is not the caricature drawn by Creighton Lacy in his essay on "The Christian Mission and a World Neighborhood," in the book *The Christian Mission Today*. There he writes of the Church standing "on the sidelines, clutching the gospel to avoid contamination" (p. 48). The Church's task is to preach the Word of God for the conversion of non-Christians and then to explain its implications for a full Christian life and the fulfilling of the cultural mandate to exercise dominion over nature as good stewards for God. Only thereby can the foundation be laid for a genuine social and economic justice.

Even men of our Western civilization, which for centuries has been under the influence of Christian teaching, will not live by lofty social principles of justice unless their lives are gripped and controlled by the inner spiritual power of the living God. The 1961 trials of the Philadelphia Electric Company executives accused of conspiring to defraud are but another illustration of this. The Church's mission to the nations must begin with preaching to them the gospel of Christ for the conversion of their lives and continue as a ministry of the whole Word of God for their growth in sanctification. Any effort to establish societies of unregenerate men on principles of social and economic justice, or to teach such principles to men not indwelt by God, will not produce the desired results. The ultimate answer to communist propaganda promising social reform is not the Church as institute agitating for it also among unregenerate men, but the Church expending every effort to move genuinely converted Christians, witnessing by life and word, to win others to Christ that they too might be empowered by His Spirit to live and work for Christian principles of justice.

Needy People and Material Relief

The temptation to be drawn aside from the basic task of the Church's mission, and to put a prior emphasis on a ministry other than that of preaching the gospel, today faces the evangelical Church as well as those who reject the Bible as their final authority. For instance, a writer in the *United Evangelical Action* has stated, "Missionaries went out at first only to save people's souls. But they discovered . . . the clamor of the physical was so great that there wasn't much opportunity for the heart and mind and soul to be engaged in meditation. So the intelligent missionary, to reach the soul of man, did something about his body." He goes on to mention such activity as opening clinics for better health, education for a better mind, agriculture for more food, and hygiene to combat disease (Judd, p. 8).

In the same edition, another writer, sent to Korea to report on relief conditions there, declares, "A starving person is in too great distress to believe in the Lord Jesus. He has to have food first. Then he will gladly consider the One in whose name the food was given." This writer also states, "The problem of supplying the minimum essentials to the millions of war-ruined Korea is beyond the combined efforts of government and relief organizations" (Haskin, p. 19).

The extent to which the Church in its mission to the nations should become involved in material relief to all needy people is a knotty problem. It is, however, one to which Christian scholars and missionaries ought to give very serious thought today before evangelical churches drift into showing greater pity for men's physical well-being than for their spiritual, or are pushed by pressure for a display of humanitarian consideration, into an unscriptural emphasis that may well restrict the advance of the gospel, the Church's immediate objective. The problem is a thorny one easily distorted by hypothetical considerations. It must be remembered, for instance, that although multitudes of Asian and African people are living on a minimum diet this does not mean that they are in the state of "a starving person in too great distress to believe in the Lord Jesus."

If the evangelical Church as institute must raise funds to feed the hungry of the world before it can preach the gospel to them, then there will be little preaching. The demand would far exceed the total contributions from their relatively limited financial resources and thus would preclude the use of funds for the support of missionaries to proclaim the gospel. We need to recall that the New Testament appeals for funds for material relief directed to the churches were for help for "the saints" or for "a sister or brother" in Christ. We should remember also that our Lord who could have fed all the hungry of His day did not do so but fed the multitudes only on two occasions when they were in dire need of food because they had followed Him into the wilderness to hear His ministry. Subsequently he refused a repetition of this feeding with the admonition, "Labor not for the meat that perisheth, but for that meat which endureth unto everlasting life" (John 6:27). If the organized Church, which cannot feed all the hungry, should get sidetracked into trying to do so in the belief that it cannot proclaim the gospel to them until they are fed, the advancement of the gospel will surely be greatly restricted.

Does this mean that the individual Christian or missionary must say to the hungry, "Go and seek help elsewhere. I only give to help preach the gospel"? Surely not. We must help those to whom we witness who are destitute of daily food, as we are able. The determining of to how many and to what extent is a difficult problem and one which needs thorough study from a biblical viewpoint. But let us not think we cannot witness to all the hungry before feeding them.

A Summary of Objectives

The true objectives of the Church's mission to the nations, and the need of the people of the world for that mission, have not changed with the changing centuries. The gospel of Christ is as relevant in the seventh decade of the 20th century as it was in the seventh decade of the first. These true objectives follow from the true biblical basis of missions that we have already considered. They are also involved in the very presentation of the Great Commission as our Lord gave it.

First, the immediate aim of the Church's mission to the nations is to make disciples of Christ from among the people of the nations through the preaching of the gospel, that they might be converted from their heathen religious beliefs to faith in Jesus Christ for the salvation of their souls, and to a walk of obedient witness for God's glory.

The second objective follows from the first and is implicit in the second part of the Great Commission; that is, to establish churches with the converts in their communities, organizing them under the oversight of their officers that full provision for their spiritual growth and evangelistic outreach might be made. The work of baptizing in the name of the Father, and the Son, and the Holy Spirit, these three who are One and who have provided for the existence of the Church and its expansion to all nations, is the work of the office bearers of the Church. The command to baptize the disciples as the gospel goes forth from nation to nation must comprehend the provision for the perpetuation of office bearers in the Church to do the work, and the Acts narrative shows us how Paul undertook this in his missionary journeys.

The new churches, although begun by the activity of others, cannot continue to lean on them but must grow as self-governing, self-supporting and self-propagating indigenous institutions. Basic to this growth must be, from the beginning, thorough grounding in all the principles of Scripture through Bible instruction in every department of the church. Evangelism itself is not an adequate goal for the Church's mission to the nations, but evangelism should be to the end of building Christ's Church through the establishing of the Church as institute. Only in this way will the continuance of the work of evangelism itself be assured.

Finally, then, the third objective of the Church's mission must be to teach all the words of Christ, all the Word of God. If the young churches are to produce the marks of the true Church they must be grounded in the Word of God by thorough teaching. If they are to spread the gospel by multiplying themselves, growing by the addition of new trophies of God's grace from the heathen world, bringing more and more men under the dominion of Christ who are aware of their cultural mandate to bring nature under their dominion for the glory of God, then the believers must be taught well, and a ministry trained to teach them. This latter is the work of seminaries such as our Japan Christian Theological Seminary in Tokyo. This is an independent institution founded on the great Westminster confessional standards and dedicated to the proposition that the Bible is the Word of the living Triune God, "the only infallible rule of faith and practice." The work of teaching those who will teach others also is basic to the establishment of a strong church in new territory.

This then is the Church's mission to the nations, the great task of the Christian Church, Christ's deep concern, and God's eternal purpose. Should not this matter of taking Christ's gospel to the foreign nations be given a top priority in the thinking of our Christian youth today? Not because it is more heroic to do so, for it isn't; or that it is a more romantic endeavor, or will evidence a more pious nature or higher spiritual level. These are but human fictions and false motives. The appeal to give priority in consideration to the foreign mission fields rests in that it is God's eternal purpose that His Church take His gospel to all the nations, and so few are doing this today. It is said that today more than 90 percent of the ordained ministers are preaching to less than 10 percent of the world's people, while less than 10 percent of the ministers are trying to reach the unevangelized multitudes in the nations where Christ is scarcely known. The true Church's effort is pathetic relative to the extent of the task.

God grant that increasingly from our sound seminaries will go forth to the nations men of the highest ability, learning and devotion: men motivated by the love of God and aiming at His glory, to fulfill His eternal purpose that Gentiles from every tribe and tongue should be made fellow members in the body of Christ, establishing churches zealously engaged in expanding the kingdom of God, for this is the true Church's mission to the nations.

Questions for Study and Discussion

1. What is the primary task of the true Church?
2. What is the ultimate ground of the Church's mission to the nations?
3. What is the "mystery" spoken of in Ephesians 3?
4. Illustrate the fact that "the Church is to propagate the Church" from the Gospels, the Acts, the Epistles, and the Revelation.
5. What are the three main objectives of missions?
6. Describe the false views of the object of missions that are held by two or more contemporary theologians.
7. To what extent should social service work be part of preaching the gospel to the nations?

Developing Self-Governing, Self-Propagating Churches

9

"The missionary should be asking the questions: Who will I leave in charge of this work? Who seems to be the one for real responsibility here? Not that he makes the final choice. He is building an indigenous church, but certainly his perception is likely to be keener than that of the young Christians."

The goal of a missionary, as our definition of missions indicated in the opening chapter, envisions the establishing of indigenous churches as a direct outgrowth of missionary endeavor. A truly indigenous church will be self-governing, self-propagating and self-supporting. This chapter will deal with the development of the first two of these in establishing indigenous churches.

Surely there are few missionary organizations that would not claim it to be their desire to see an indigenous church established from their missionary efforts. On the contrary, most missionary organizations not only desire to see such a result from their missionary labors but also set this as one of the major goals for each of their fields. Mission boards are organized, and missionaries go abroad to foreign fields, with the desire to win converts to Christ. It is difficult to imagine their not wanting to see sufficient numbers of converts won so that these can arrange their own affairs and give sufficiently of their time and means to insure the preaching of God's Word both to themselves and to their whole neighborhood. The indigenous church is thus accepted almost everywhere among missions and missionaries as the ideal goal, although one exceptionally difficult to achieve.

What, however, is an indigenous church? It has been pointed out that "In common usage, an indigenous church is defined as a church that is self-governing, self-supporting, and self-propagating" (Soltau, *Missions,* p.24). A fuller definition offered is, "Applied to missionary work, the word indigenous means that, as a result of missionary effort, a native church has been produced which shares the life of the country in which it is planted and finds within itself the ability to govern itself, support itself, and reproduce itself" (Hodges, p. 7).

Some have objected to what they have called the emphasis on "self" in this terminology. One missionary churchman, for instance, has written, "It is much to be regretted that such a matter should have been far too long tied up to 'self.' 'Self'—whether it is referred to support, government, or extension—is not the highest ideal. The Church must take the place of 'self'; so that the ideal before the churches—younger and older—ought to be Church-support, Church-government and Church-extension." (Azariah, p. 367).

At one point, however, perhaps an addition could profitably be made to the fuller definition of the indigenous church. A native church must not only share in the life of the country, but, to be a true church, it must have Christ's life within its members. There are native churches founded on erroneous concepts of Christ and His gospel that have reached self-support and self-government and, to a measure, are self-propagating. It is in this last named area, however, that the church without the inner life of Christ will most readily be seen to fall short of its goal. Without the indwelling Christ, a church may carry His name but will lack the motivating power to do its utmost to spread His gospel. Thus an indigenous church is considered here to be a body of believers organized for worship, the edification of the saints, and the spread of the gospel, planted in a soil foreign to the gospel until the arrival of missionaries through whose labors a native church was produced, founded upon Jesus Christ as He is offered in the Scriptures, sharing the life of the land, self-governing, self-supporting, and self-propagating from devotion to Christ, and aiming at the extension of His kingdom.

How to Build an Indigenous Church

Our first consideration is this: How does one begin an indigenous church? How is the work started in order to build an indigenous church in a foreign mission land? The first objective and essential beginning is the making of disciples (Matt. 28:19a). Without converts there could be no church. The first aim then is to win converts to Jesus Christ. Since there is no one prescribed method of doing this a number of tried and proven ways will be mentioned. One, which has proved very satisfactory in many lands, is street preaching. It is simply a matter of going to a suitable street location and proclaiming Christ, with some native Christians to sing and give out tracts, with the address of the regular place of meeting stamped upon the tracts. Street meetings are most effective when conducted in connection with a church location in order that the converts or interested people can be told of a place where regular meetings will be held where they can hear more of the gospel.

The Presbyterian church in Yokkaichi, about 300 miles south of Tokyo, the first church begun by the Japan Presbyterian Mission, was started by such efforts. In 1949, during our first spring there, a fellow missionary and I used to go out in the afternoon to hold street meetings in the city. We had been holding Children for Christ meetings in our home from January to April of 1949. Many children had come to learn the required Bible verses and received the New Testament awarded. It had raised some interest in their homes, so we decided to have a street meeting near Ise Hachioji Station, a short distance from our rented house.

We chose the day of a Shinto festival to set up a jeep, with loud speaker equipment, at the bottom of a long flight of stone stairs leading up to the shrine. It was an open area, so, when the people came down from the shrine, we had quite an audience. Of those present at that particular meeting, however, I know of no individual who came to our church service at the address stamped on the tract. A junior high school girl who happened to go by, however, took one of the tracts home, and her older brother read it. He was a young man of about 20 who ran a farm for his father and also attended night high school.

He became very interested and the next Sunday morning came to our Sunday school for our first adult Bible class. From then on, he came regularly and later was converted. Today he is an elder in the church and an outstanding servant of the Lord there. It is obvious that we never know what may eventually result from such a meeting. Many illustrations could be given by missionaries of such indirect fruit.

Another method of evangelism is children's work, a very effective means of making friends in a community. People all over the world love their children with a very strong devotion, and we are interested in anyone who is interested in them. We have found it a very effective entree into homes in Japan. Our church in Matsunoki, in western Tokyo, originated out of children's work. We moved to Tokyo from Yokkaichi and started "Children for Christ" classes in October 1919. Adult meetings were started the next spring and some began to attend. The Sunday school was very large; it usually is in Japan when meetings are started for the first time, and other adults were contacted through it. The children's work, of course, should be geared both to win children and to reach their parents.

Tent evangelism is another very effective method of evangelism. It has been used effectively throughout the Far East. One of my friends in the Philippines says it is their most effective method of starting churches. It has been used in Korea from earliest missionary days. A great advantage of this method is that it solves the difficult problem of a suitable location where people can come without embarrassment. The novelty of seeing a white man come to the village to speak in a tent is sure to attract some who would not come to a home or hall. Kenzo Uchimura, a famous early Japanese convert, has written an amusing description of his first attendance at a Christian meeting. He said a friend invited him to come to hear a "pretty woman sing, and a tall big man with a long beard shout and howl upon an elevated place, flinging his arms and twisting his body in all fantastic manners, to all which admittance is entirely free. . . . Sunday after Sunday . . . sightseeing, and not truth seeking, was the only view I had" (Uchimura, p. 14). He went to see this great curiosity and that was his first introduction to Christianity!

Our church in Hachioji, a suburb of Tokyo, was started in the summer of 1957 through a tent meeting. Some of the students and a missionary went out there for a series of meetings. Although there were only a few converts, a meeting place was found and meetings were continued with student help all that winter. The next summer they went out again for another series of meetings and this time more were saved including a communist nurse, a party member, who proved a great help by contributing generously of her funds to the church for the pastor's support. The third summer a store was rented at a central place for three weeks. The meetings were held through that summer in 1959, and more converts were won. People have been saved and a church founded as a result of this tent evangelism.

The English Bible class too has proved very effective. Doubtless the effectiveness of this method differs in various countries, but the urge to learn English exists throughout Asia. In Japan, if a class is advertised to be in English, immediately there is a good response from students who want to listen to English. Frequently in Oriental lands they have learned English from their own people. Thus, when they come in contact with someone from an English-speaking nation, they find the accent different and difficult to understand. They speak of their "hearing" being poor, in other words, they cannot comprehend what is said because they are used to hearing English spoken in their own, frequently erroneous, accent. Because they are to listen to a native American or Englishman talk in his own tongue, they will come to the English Bible class to improve their hearing. English is the bait, and this is understood both by the missionary and those who come. They agree that they will make the Bible the subject matter for study and discussion. The Lord works through His Word, and as they have heard it week after week many young people have been won to Christ through these English Bible classes. After they really become interested and want to find out more, they will discuss Christian matters in their own language in order to receive fuller understanding. A number of the young people who have come to our seminary in Tokyo were saved in such English Bible classes.

The problem that rises immediately when converts are made is: Where shall we meet? What shall we use for a meeting place? An important decision faces the missionary. The missionary can start the meetings in his own home. We have done that in the past, but I think I have learned that it is not really the best way. We did it in Ise Hachioji before we moved to Tokyo. By the overruling providence of God, it was effective there, however, because the year the church was started, we pulled out and left it there! The landlady from whom we rented was one of the first converts, so our departure after ten months left the church meeting in her home, a "church in the house" as the early New Testament churches were. The people paid her rent and also for the utilities. She was a widow living in a large house alone and the first floor was very well adapted for church use.

In Tokyo, however, where we again started a church in our home, but from which we did not plan to move, problems arose in time. We felt the church would make more progress in self-dependence and influencing outsiders to come if it had its own meeting place. We feared the people would develop a spirit of dependence upon the missionary, dependence upon the things he was supplying in the home, such as lights, facilities, and the security of knowing a place of worship existed because he had supplied it. The dependent spirit is the easiest thing in the world to develop and one of the hardest things to break. It is wise to be conscious of this from the very beginning and to try to avoid it. To supply one's home and all the facilities for the young church is a temptation as the easiest way but it may well prove not to be the best thing for the growth of the church in numbers or spirituality. They, too, must learn to rely not on man but on the Lord. Halls can usually be rented for Sunday meetings. Frequently, places can be found that are used six days of the week but are not used on Sundays, such as private sewing schools or abacus schools where children learn to use the abacus in the evening. If one tries hard enough, usually some such place can be found. Of course, if there is a convert who owns his own home this can be a happy solution. In such a case, the neighbors often become interested, and the work gets an encouraging start.

After the converts are made and the meetings are started, another serious problem arises. Who shall be baptized, and who will do the baptizing? Pre-baptism classes are absolutely essential. There is a great difference of opinion, however, as to how much knowledge a new convert should be required to have before he is baptized. Some insist on a wide knowledge of doctrine, going considerably beyond a clear profession of salvation, before the converts can become members of the church.

What then should be established as a rule of practice in the mission land? The missionary certainly must insist on a clear understanding of the way of salvation and see that there is clear comprehension of the general doctrinal picture of the Bible, a clear understanding of the Triune God, the Bible as God's revelation, creation, man, sin, idolatry, salvation, the Person and work of Christ, the indwelling Holy Spirit, the Church, its support, Christian life, etcetera.

One point where the prospective members need to be interrogated very, very carefully is on the subject of idolatry. If the head of the house has a god shelf in his home, what shall be required? Such things have to be destroyed by a believer who has responsibility for them. If he is not responsible, that is, if he is not the head of the home, then he may not be able to have them removed, but it is his responsibility to have no participation at all in any worship of polytheistic symbols or in heathen festivals. The new converts must be carefully trained and interrogated about these things that they might know that God demands a separation from all worship that is not worship of Himself.

Church attendance and financial support of the church also need emphasis. In some countries there is a strong tradition of supporting the churches. In others, like Japan, there is a weak tradition, and this matter of giving must be emphasized. So too with witnessing. In Korea some churches have as one of the tests for baptism the question, "Have you won someone to the Lord?" Others take the position that the converts must at least give evidence they are trying to win someone to the Lord. They are required to give the names of some to whom they have witnessed and those whom they are actually trying to win.

These then are some of the areas of instruction for those who are preparing for baptism. How long should they receive the instruction before they are baptized? Generally speaking, in Japan we say three to six months should be allowed from the time one has made a clear-cut confession of Christ as Savior before he is baptized. What do we look for in those three to six months? Certainly a gaining of this knowledge of which we have been speaking, a growth in knowledge of doctrine and in spiritual life, in other words, clear evidence that this individual really is walking and growing with Jesus Christ.

If the missionary is beginning a new church, the presence of new converts raises still another question: Who is going to do the baptizing? The missionary, of course, if he is the one who has led the early converts to Christ in a new area, is the pastor for the time being. He should, however, try to make it his goal to remove himself from that position as soon as possible. It is easy to succumb to the temptation of becoming anchored down as the pastor of one little congregation even though one has planned to bring the gospel to as wide an area as possible. The missionary evangelist to a new area, however, ought not to be tied down only to one place. He ought to seek to get a church started, get it on its feet, and try to start another somewhere else.

If a missionary starts the church, then it is assumed he will do the initial training and interrogating for the baptism. But he must be looking for those who can assume responsibility for the group right there among them. Sometimes this is a great problem, but frequently it is not. If there are any men among the believers, the possibility of leadership is present.

The missionary should be asking the questions: Who will I leave in charge of this work? Who seems to be the one for real responsibility here? Not that he makes the final choice. He is building an indigenous church, but certainly his perception is likely to be keener than that of the young Christians. His leadership, being the original leadership, will be accepted to a great extent by them. The one he approves will in all likelihood be the one to whom they respond, unless his comprehension of the situation is very faulty. While he is teaching, as the first baptisms are made, and as he is watching these young people or these new converts develop, he must keep the question of future leadership before him.

How to Build a Self-Governing Church

This brings us then to the next issue, the organization of this self-governing church. With baptized converts in existence, the point is reached where organization must be considered. Officers, those responsible for carrying on the work so the missionary can put his interest and time elsewhere, must be selected. If the church is to select them, it must be organized to some extent in order to do it and to provide a framework within which the officers can function. But how will it be organized? The Bible ought to be where we look for an answer as we try to find out how the church should be organized.

If we are to look into the Bible to see how God has governed His people through history, we must first take notice of the nature with which God constituted man and of man's subsequent fall. By creation man was constituted a rational, religious, and responsible being, as has been pointed out in an earlier chapter, with true knowledge, holiness, and righteousness. In the Fall, man, though retaining the first three, lost the latter three and, as Paul points out, in his regeneration is renewed in these (Col. 3:10; Eph. 4:24). In order that renewed men might grow in knowledge, holiness, and righteousness and realize more fully something of their lost potential as rational, religious, and responsible beings, God provided three orders of offices to help them. He gave them first prophets to bring them knowledge of God, priests to lead them to holiness, and kings to rule and judge them that they might live righteously in an orderly society.

When our Lord Jesus Christ came, He had these three offices within Himself, being anointed by His Father to be our Prophet, Priest, and King (Acts 3:22; Heb. 2:17; John 18:37). Prior to His ascension, Jesus passed these offices on to His chosen apostles for the governing of His Church (John 20:21-23).

The apostles were thus the first temporary officers of the New Testament church. Who did they put in charge of the work? We find three types of officers set forth in the New Testament. The first ones mentioned are in Acts 6, the deacons, who were given the oversight of mercy or relief. Now some say that the deacons should be allowed to take over the work of the ruling elders and that ruling elders, as a separate office, are no longer necessary. Yet all we have to do is to look at the later epistles of Paul, Timothy, and Titus, to see his emphasis on both the offices of deacons and ruling elders. Scriptural justification for the idea that the deacons take the place of the elders, or can assume their ruling ministry, cannot be found. Both offices appear in Scripture right up to the end of the epistles.

In Acts 14:23, the first mention of the Gentile elders appears. In the twelfth chapter there are some elders mentioned in Jerusalem, but the probability is that these were the elders of the Jewish church, perhaps carried over as converts from the Jewish synagogue. Certainly here in Acts 14, however, we see elders ordained by Paul in his Gentile ministry. We read that he ordained elders in every church, commended them to the Lord on whom they believed, passed on through Pisidia, came to Pamphylia, and so on. Paul certainly sought out responsible men to be elders and set them in the place of that responsibility.

Who then were the bishops? We find them spoken of in the Acts narrative and elsewhere in the New Testament. Acts 20 sheds some light on the respective meanings of these two terms. In Acts 20:17, we read, "And from Miletus he sent to Ephesus, and called the elders of the church." Then we turn to verse 28 and read, "Take heed therefore unto yourselves, and to all the flock, over the which the Holy Ghost hath made you overseers [made you bishops], to feed the church of God." The elders were the bishops. The same men were designated by both these terms. Why then were two words used? One reason perhaps was because of the national backgrounds. The Jews referred to their spiritual rulers as "elders" (*presbuteros*) and the Greeks, to whom Paul was preaching in Acts, used the term "bishop" (*episcopos*), overseer. This latter word was used some centuries earlier by the Athenians to designate their appointed small city administrators.

One term probably emphasizes the office and the other the work. We could turn to other places, such as the first chapter of Titus, and again see that these words, bishop and elder, are used interchangeably (Titus 1:5, 7). The word "elder" seems to point to the maturity and dignity of the office and "bishop" to the actual work of overseeing. The qualifications of elders, who also must be "apt to teach," are given in 1 Timothy 3:1-7; Titus 1:5-9, and 1 Peter 5:1-5.

Finally, we come to the third office, the office of the preaching elder, or the minister. The special office of the ministry increased in prominence as the era of the apostles closed. The apostolic office lasted only for their own lifetime. The preaching elders, whose main task was to take up the preaching ministry being laid down by the apostles, appear during this apostolic period. Theirs is a dual office both of preaching and ruling. In 1 Timothy 5:17, we read, "Let the elders that rule well be counted worthy of double honor, especially they who labor in the word and doctrine." The ruling elders by virtue of their office were responsible for the spiritual government of the church although they must also be able to teach (Heb. 13:17; 1 Peter 5:1-3). But there were others, the preaching elders, whose office made them responsible both to teach the Word of God and to share in the ruling. Our Lord thus provided for the continuance of these special offices after the apostles' departure by appointing the permanent offices of deacons, to administer the mercy of God (Acts 6:2-6); ruling elders, to administer God's spiritual oversight of His Church (Acts 14:23; Heb. 13:17); and preaching elders or ministers, to administer the Word of God and share in the spiritual ruling (1 Tim. 4:14, 5:17; 2 Tim. 4:2-5; Rev. 2:1ff).

Paul refers to himself in another place (1 Cor. 4:1) as a "minister of Christ." The preaching elder certainly was that; he was the minister of the Word of God, the servant of God serving the Word of God in his spiritual ministry. This is and ought to be the example we have before us as we seek to build indigenous churches in foreign lands. Paul, the missionary and apostle, set before us the offices to govern Christ's church and the example of their appointment, and gave us the criteria by which to judge a man to see if he has the gifts and calling of these offices. It ought not to be too great a problem to know who should be an elder or deacon if we judge by the qualifications Paul speaks of in 1 Timothy 3:1-13. If men have these gifts from God, they are qualified for the office, and this is indicative that God intended them to use these gifts that He has given. Both the elders and the deacons are mentioned in that long passage.

Again in Titus 1:5 we read, "For this cause left I thee in Crete, that thou shouldest set in order the things that are wanting, and ordain elders in every city. . . ." Here is Paul recalling his instructions to his young protégé as he provided for building Christ's church among the nations. Titus is to "ordain elders in every city as I had appointed thee." Paul then related the criteria for an elder. "If any be blameless, the husband of one wife, having faithful children not accused of riot or unruly. For a bishop must be blameless," (here then are the two words, verse 5, the "elder," and, verse 7, the "bishop") "as the steward of God; not self-willed, not soon angry, not given to wine, no striker, not given to filthy lucre; But a lover of hospitality, a lover of good men, sober, just, holy, temperate; Holding fast the faithful word as he has been taught, that he may be able by sound doctrine both to exhort and to convince the gainsayers."

In 2 Timothy 2:2, we find Paul urging Timothy, "And the things that thou hast heard of me among many witnesses, the same commit thou to faithful men, who shall be able to teach others also." He urged the selection of such men to perpetuate the work, and this the missionary must do also by seeing that they are selected. The calling comes from God; the appointment, their designation, comes from God's people. The missionary must be careful to avoid, however, the development of the dependent spirit at this point. He is not wise if his method is simply to say to them, "This is your best man, let him be the elder." Better to sit down with the congregation, consult with them about the nature of their need for an elder, study together and let them give their opinions. If it is obvious that a particular man is the logical one, let them be the ones who suggest it. In this way self-government can develop rather than having a spirit of authoritarianism and dictatorship grow from the missionary's method. The leadership must develop from them.

Now, how does a man who is a relatively unlearned farmer, like that farmer in Yokkaichi, develop into a wise elder in a church? It does not come instantly, but through Bible training and spiritual growth. Let him be a Sunday School teacher first, for instance, which will make him study the Bible even more thoroughly. It makes him a teacher. As he gets better at it, let him teach the adults. Then let the missionary be absent a Sunday, first arranging for various ones to conduct the service. They may be very reluctant to do it if he is there, but if he is away they will go ahead and do what has to be done. In this way they gain experience and confidence, and the work goes forward. In six months' or eight months' time, the man may already have demonstrated that he has the ability and the calling of the Lord for this work and can be set to it. Perhaps it might be wise to give him a temporary office for six months or one year at first, as a testing period, and if it then seems justified let him be ordained after that. The Scriptures have numerous instructions advocating cautious procedure. "Prove all things" (1 Thess. 5:21). "Lay hands [of ordination, see 4:14] suddenly on no man" (1 Tim. 5:22). "And let these also first be proved; then let them use the office of a deacon, being found blameless" (1 Tim. 3:10). There is one thing which should be emphasized here. The missionary ought to avoid paying men who volunteer their services to the Lord and give part of their time each week to the work of the church. An elder who gives his time for visitation or gives some of his time for lay evangelism is doing it unto the Lord. This is the way it should be, but if a precedent is established of a missionary reimbursing him for this kind of voluntary service it can be an impediment to the growth of the church. Others may come and say, "I want to be a Christian," but later it will become clear that what they really wanted was the paid job. The non-paid, regular members will feel their efforts are unwanted or are unnecessary as paid men are doing the witnessing. Many unhappy results can follow such an unwise practice. A man who is getting this salary may not be satisfied, and if someone else will give him more may go to him to get it. Further, to pay a promising Christian to leave a church to work elsewhere will be a real loss to his home church, which needs him in this early stage of its development. The church must be self-supporting, self-propagating, and self-governing from the beginning and the missionary must give encouragement, not discouragement, to this growth.

Bible classes for the careful instructing of elders and Sunday School teachers are an important means of developing them. In Korea, an agricultural country, these were carefully planned for the winter months so farmers could attend in their slack season. Bible institutes of three weeks' or six weeks' duration were conducted for teacher training and elder leadership development. They were given systematic Bible and doctrinal instruction, as well as training in Christian life, church government, administration of finances, and other matters relevant to church leadership.

If outstanding leadership is to be produced in the church, real effort must be made to produce it, and these seasonal Bible institutes can make a great contribution. The church must be led to develop the true marks of the Church of Jesus Christ, that is, faithful preaching of the Word, proper administration of the sacraments, and the correct administration of discipline. Faithful teaching is essential to produce and maintain these marks.

The matter of discipline needs special emphasis because of the natural human tendency to avoid unpleasantness. There is thus inevitably a strong impulse to be lax towards those who are in error rather than to try to correct them. Christ, however, gave careful instructions concerning the maintaining of discipline and entrusted discipline to the officers of His Church (John 20:23; Matt. 18:17-18). If the church is faithfully and systematically to discharge its obligation of disciplining offenders, then it must have an organized government and specified standards by which its officers can be guided in their maintaining of it. If discipline is not undertaken from the very beginning, only tragic results can follow. The people must be taught from the beginning, "Here are our standards, our doctrinal standards and our standards for Christian life. Willful disregard of them must be disciplined."

The purpose of discipline, as stated in the *Book of Discipline of the Westminster Standards* is "to vindicate the honor of Christ, to promote the purity of His Church, and to reclaim the offender." If someone deviates from the church's essential standards for faith and life, he must be dealt with. If he won't change, but insists on continuing in his way, contrary to what God has set forth, then he must be disciplined.

Who does the disciplining? Many missionaries have made a mistake at this point, for they have tried to do it themselves. Of course it would be better to have them do it than no one do it. But let us look at Paul's example in 1 Corinthians 5:11-13. He did not go to that Corinthian church and say, "Look, I am going to remove this man from your membership. I'm putting this fornicator out." Rather he stayed away and urged them by letter to discipline the man before he came. After it was done, the man repented and changed (2 Cor. 2:6-8). The problem is, if the missionary does the disciplining, he is not letting the church bear its responsibilities. Further, if anti-foreignism is present in the neighborhood, the disciplined one may use it to confuse the whole issue.

More than that, the missionary is very likely to make a mistake if he acts alone. He is much less likely to know all the background of the problem than the people of his church. He may have a wrong grasp of the situation. The elders are in a far better position to handle it, and when they do, and the church stands together, the people do not receive the impression that an outsider has intervened. By letting the church itself handle it, although they may have to be pushed to do it, there is a far greater possibility of understanding and sympathy with the act of discipline. This, of course, is a very important factor. To handle the matter this way is to follow the scriptural precedent set forth by Paul.

How to Build a Self-Propagating Church

The missionary should have a great concern not only to see a self-governing church organized but a self-propagating one also. How then can the attaining of this goal of self-propagation be furthered? It should be natural and spontaneous, since life wants to reproduce itself, that the new life in the church should want to produce new life also. Joy in sharing joy is a natural way for the Christian gospel to be spread. Multiplication comes by one learning and then teaching others, each of whom must teach many others again. If lay evangelists are to be produced, a purposeful effort must be made to train the people to be such. Great emphasis upon every Christian being a witness is necessary with the pastor or the missionary first making it and then going on to train the elders and people to see and make opportunities for themselves for starting a Sunday school here, a child evangelism class there, or going to the next village to start something there. Every church should be seeking to multiply itself and to produce another church. It is the church's task to reproduce the church by the grace of God.

Some national churches have had amazing success in this extension work. In Korea, we heard of a church that had divided itself three times, not the kind of sad divisions we have too often in our home churches, but a church agreeing to have a group of its people leave to start a branch work in another area. This one mother church by this means has produced three others since the War. In El Salvador, it is reported that in one place, within a radius of 20 miles of the first church, something like 25 other churches have started as a result of every individual being a witness for the Lord and lay evangelists going out to proclaim the gospel! (Hodges, p. 40)

In the early life of the church there must be a constant emphasis on this matter of expanding the dominion of Christ through self-propagation of the church. The missionary must not only teach but set the example to the new converts by his day-to-day house visitation, tract distribution, street meetings, and visits to other villages. Colored slides of the life of Christ or of biblical stories, shown in open places on an evening, provide an excellent means of introducing the gospel to a new community. Young converts find it easy on such occasions to give out tracts and invite people to come to their Sunday services. Weeknight Bible classes to teach the young converts methods of witnessing the message, as well as its content, are very helpful. The sermons and prayers of the missionary should also reflect the vital Christian concern for reaching the lost and bringing the rule of Christ to all the world. A missionary must always remember the task is far greater than he can handle alone and that the most effective method of multiplying his effort is to train many others to work with him in it.

The matter of a sound system of doctrine is extremely important also, for pastors need to be trained in the whole counsel of God, the whole Word of God systematically understood, a well-integrated confession of faith, not just in a few Bible doctrines viewed independently from their relation to the whole. The history of the origin of the Nihon Kirisuto Kyokai, product of the first Presbyterian work in Japan, which eventually developed into the wartime Nihon Kirisuto Kyodan, United Church of Japan, shows the sad result of an inadequate doctrinal foundation. Back in 1890, Uemura, one of the early Presbyterian pastors, urged them to give up the *Westminster Confession*. He did this on the grounds that a young church first needed a simple creed and that later, as they grew, they would develop their own confession of faith. Much against the advice of Dr. Hepburn, one of the first Presbyterian missionaries, and some of the others, the church voted to give up the *Westminster Confession* and take the *Apostles' Creed*, plus a few simple statements in addition, as their total creed. Their expectation was to develop from this simple creed to a comprehensive one. But this never eventuated. We cannot turn our backs on what the Holy Spirit has done through 1,900 years and go forward. God has led men in these confessional statements. He has led them into a deeper and deeper understanding of His truth, His Word, which is not to say that He has led them into an understanding of the total truth. But we cannot go forward by going backward to the beginning and trying to start all over again as if the Holy Spirit had done nothing in the intervening centuries.

Within 17 years from the time Uemura got the church to give up the *Westminster Confession*, that is from 1890 to 1907, the seminary of the N.K.K. went over to modernist teaching and one of the Southern Presbyterian missionaries had to lead a large group of students out to start a new, sound seminary. It is a fatal mistake not to have a clear, strong, biblical confession for faith and life behind the start of a church—it is my firm conviction. Those churches that have started and continued with one, like the Korean Presbyterian Church, have maintained a stability and consistency of purpose in spite of tremendous pressures put on them over the years.

In addition to training these young pastors in a thorough understanding of the Bible and its system of doctrine, a special emphasis must be made in those areas where there is a tendency to be weak because of cultural or national background. The young Japanese pastor, for instance, needs to be trained to be what Professor Yanagita has called "the wrestling-type Christian." This expression has a good biblical basis (Eph. 6:12; 2 Tim. 2:3; 4:7). The man who will be forthright in his presentation, who for love of Christ will wrestle against compromise of doctrine or life or against idolatry or any of the things that compromise the Christian testimony, is the man Christ's Church needs today. To produce such men ought to be a major objective in training pastors. Evangelistic preachers and workers must have this spirit. In Japan, too, often one finds what is called a "sensei complex," the "teacher complex." It is very easy to get that complex. The teacher is one who sits down and people come to him for instruction. But that is not doing "the work of an evangelist." An evangelist has to go out to the people. In an Oriental land where a teacher's position is held in high esteem, it is very easy for one attaining the position of a pastor to fall into this "teacher complex" type of thinking. The long Buddhist tradition in which the priests made no effort to reach others but simply let the people come to them if they wished, is also behind this complex. Such a view has to be wrestled with, too, in order to be counteracted if young men are to become genuinely evangelistic in their efforts.

The "club complex" is another erroneous view to be counteracted. The "club complex," the idea that the church is "our" private society, "our group," with the result that an outsider is not made to feel at home, is not foreign to some churches in America either. The stranger is thought of as an outsider, so instead of being welcomed in an evangelistic spirit, the group stays together and enjoys its wonderful fellowship without making any real effort to bring him in. The "club complex" develops. This is certainly something we have to guard against.

A missionary from China in Japan, after working in Japan some years, said to me one day, "You know, it seems to me our Japanese churches have 'fiftyitis.'"

I asked in surprise, "What is 'fiftyitis'?"

He replied, "They get up to fifty and that is as far as they can go. They can't go beyond fifty."

The average membership of an evangelical church in Japan is said to be about 40. Before churches reach 50, some trouble arises; there are divisions and people fall away. Few churches seem able to get beyond that. An indigenous evangelical church must develop the sense of being one family in Christ with its members ready to suppress personal difference for the peace and unity of the church that schisms may not come. They need that vision of evangelism, of genuine concern for the lost and feeling of responsibility to spread the Word, and then the growth will come.

The missionary's or pastor's effort at personal evangelism among lost men, women, and children should also aim at instilling this concern for others into his own people. Concern for others is not a characteristic of the heathen. There are many instances of church members bringing their many problems to their pastor and so overwhelming him with interviews and subsequent negotiations on their behalf that the pastor literally had no time for evangelism. The people must be trained to do as Peter has recommended, "Casting all your care upon him; for he careth for you" (1 Pet. 5:7). If a pastor tries to be the sole burden-bearer for all his people, which sometimes to me seems to be the Japanese church members' concept of a pastor, he will neither do them nor his Lord a service. The Christian, like a child, must learn to stand on his own feet before the Lord. The pastor must be free to give considerable time to the work of evangelism. This is a prime necessity for a self-propagating church. The pastor must have time to work with the covenant children of the church, training them in sound doctrine, as well as seeking to reach the children outside the church. Certainly, he must also look for keen young people in his church to work with him in these efforts. The prayer meeting can be an effective instrument in developing concern for the salvation of lost people and for the expansion of the ministry of the church as the pastor leads his people to pray specifically for these goals. The conversion of those for whom the church is praying is a great encouragement and stimulus for more prayer and work.

The people must also constantly have held before them the relation between their financial contributions and their evangelistic outreach. In many Oriental countries there is a long tradition of a great gulf being fixed between spiritual things and financial matters. The result is that pastors are frequently very reluctant to mention money or the need of the church increasing its giving. Not so was it with Paul. "Let him that is taught in the Word communicate [give gifts] unto him that teacheth in all good things," he wrote to the Galatians (6:6). Again, "Even so hath the Lord ordained that they which preach the gospel should live of the gospel" (1 Cor. 9:14). The people must be brought to see that it is by their giving to the support of the pastor and the church's evangelistic work that the gospel of Jesus Christ will reach others and bring them into His Church (2 Cor. 9:6-8). This realization and concern for the lost will be a far greater incentive to giving than a mere sense of duty.

The New Testament church was a self-propagating church. The missionary church today must also be one, constantly aiming at reaching others and starting new churches. The New Testament church was a self-governing church. It was self-governing in order to do its work as a church, not just because it desired to be independent of the missionary's influence. Such independence will not in itself enable a church to fulfill its task. It will not even help the church to fulfill it unless the church has a real understanding of what its task is and a deep concern to be seeking to accomplish it. The development of this understanding and concern must be the missionary's aim as he seeks to build self-governing and self-propagating indigenous churches that the gospel may go out to all and the kingdom of Christ be expanded.

Questions for Study and Discussion

1. What is the most important characteristic of a true Christian church?
2. For what three principal functions is a church organized?
3. How does a missionary begin an indigenous church?
4. Where should a new church meet to hold its services?
5. What are some possible requirements for the baptism of a new convert?
6. What three main offices appear in New Testament church government?
7. What are some of the requirements for the baptism of a new convert?
8. What are some of the requirements for holding a church office?

9. What is the purpose of church discipline?
10. What are some of the pitfalls to be avoided if a church is to be self-propagating?

10

Developing the Self-Supporting Church

One of the major problems for the missionary as he sees converts grow, and works and prays for the establishment of an indigenous church, is the question as to what extent he should use his foreign funds to advance the work. Some missions follow the policy of going into a community to erect a church building and placing a paid pastor in it to conduct meetings, with the hope that an indigenous church will eventually result from it. Others have followed the policy of no donated buildings but freely paying native workers to operate gospel halls and do itinerant evangelism. Others again have followed the practice of not using foreign funds for either payment of buildings or pastors' salaries. The former two would probably be ready to support the thesis, "There is many a local church where self-support has been such a be-all and end-all of existence that all spirit of evangelism has been successfully smothered" (Azariah, p. 365). The latter, however, would rejoin that if self-support is such a static concept, "a be-all and end-all," it would indicate that the dynamic inner life, the activating power of the life of Christ, was missing and this was the real cause of the lack of evangelism, not the goal of self-support. Where a church is truly founded on Christ and knows and believes the message of the Bible, its motive for self-support will be that the Word may be preached to its people and to their neighbors, as far out as they can reach, through evangelism.

It is this matter of self-support, that is, of the financial support of the indigenous church, with which we are primarily concerned here. It has been rightly observed that "strictly speaking, the word [self-support] ought to be applied to a church only when all the legitimate needs and activities of a church or a congregation—pastoral, educational, evangelistic, and philanthropic—are supported by itself without any outside help. Partial support is not self-support" (Azariah, p. 362). Partial support, however, when self-support is envisioned in the complete sense of this definition, is far better than full support, especially when the goal is complete self-support and is being striven for. In that case, if the four areas of church activity given above were listed in a different arrangement they might represent the chronological order by which a native church could expect to become self-supporting in the complete sense—that is, pastoral, evangelistic, philanthropic, and educational. The missionary, gathering the first converts, would himself be the first pastor, but, as they grew, soon he would lead them in choosing one of their own to shepherd them. Together they would seek to evangelize the lost, help the poor, and give Christian education to their own. The last areas in which a native church could be expected to become fully self-supporting would be that of general education, through secondary, higher, and theological institutions. As the missionary faces this situation of the growing church, then, he must decide at many points what are the proper and what the improper use of his foreign funds in the development of an indigenous church.

Native vs. Foreign Funding

The 19th century Presbyterian missionary and scholar, John L. Nevius, whose name today is generally associated with the new system of church extension as over against the old one in which foreign funds were freely used, has described the difference between the two systems as follows: "These two systems may be distinguished in general by the former [the old] depending largely on paid native agency, while the latter deprecates and seeks to minimize such agency. . . . The relative advantages of these systems may be determined by two tests—adaptability to the end in view, and Scripture authority" (Nevius, p. 8). There is obviously no scriptural example of paying converts to help evangelize, which certainly does not preclude it in the light of Luke 10:7 ("the laborer is worthy of his hire"), but as Nevius points out there is admonition against using them too quickly or pushing them out of their calling into a new one. "A bishop then must be blameles . . . apt to teach . . . not a novice, lest being lifted up with pride he fall into the condemnation of the devil" (1 Tim. 3:2, 6). Again, "Lay hands suddenly on no man" (1 Tim. 5:22). Further, "Let every man abide in the same calling wherein he was called" (1 Cor. 7:20).

As far as the other test is concerned, however, that of the adaptability of the end in view of establishing indigenous churches, the weight of testimony against the missionary paying converts to do the work of evangelism or pastoring the churches he has begun, is quite formidable. As early as 1890, Nevius could give an impressive list of reasons and illustrations demonstrating the harmful effects of such a practice. Two generations later, a missionary conference, representing most of the older denominations whose foreign missions had to a great extent followed the old system, was presented with a report which began as follows:

> Within a year I have heard in several of the countries of Eastern Asia the remark, "I sometimes wish we could begin all over again with a different use of foreign money." This was not the comment of young missionaries, but of veterans, in the light of a generation of effort to establish the Church of Christ. Behind this comment is the realization of a neglect of elemental laws controlling growth of power, incentives to action, self-discipline and self-respect. In this area are found the mainsprings that control the development of the infant Church no less than that of the infant child. It is as futile to expect a Church to develop more than a flabby, uncertain life on the basis of a generation of external support, as to expect a strong man or woman to result from a similar course of treatment. The same principles are involved and the same laws in each case are broken. With the infant Church an indefinite period of external financial support is a further neglect of law, because the Church is composed of groups of mature persons who have made more or less satisfactory adjustments to their environment, while the human infant has to spend its first decade in making these adjustments. (Davis, *The Economic Basis of the Church*, p. 128)

The conference itself passed a number of recommendations concerning church support, including the following, which bore clear witness to their ultimate conclusion of the ineffectiveness of the old system:

> We recommend: that a courageous change of policies be made in the method of granting financial aid to the younger churches, so that the church will still be able to carry on its essential program even if outside subsidy should cease entirely. That in opening up new fields the principle of placing new groups of Christians upon their own resources for the support of their own work be applied from the very beginning. That due emphasis be placed upon the responsibility of the church in every place both to undertake its own financial support and to contribute toward community service. (p. 551)

Pastors' Salaries

The harmful effects of foreign funds being used to pay the salaries of pastors or evangelists can be seen in the experience of many missions in the different areas of relationships within the church during its development. This can first be illustrated in the area of the church members themselves. When foreign funds are used to provide the pastor for a church group, such support almost inevitably fosters a dependent spirit among the people. It weakens them, because it relieves them of the necessity of using their own resources to the fullest to forward the work for which God has made them responsible. One experienced observer in China has written: "A church once accustomed to dependence is one least attracted to independence. Dependence is natural to the child, but it is not to the church, for the latter is often most virile in its infancy whilst the former is always feeble then. We must start right" (Clark, S. J. W., p. 16).

A veteran missionary to Korea has stated:

> It cannot be overemphasized that, regardless of the social and economic standards of the people, it should be understood that they are able to bear this responsibility [self-support] unaided from the very beginning....The amount of the salaries should be decided by the national church. The people themselves are in a far better position to know how much it takes to support an individual than does the foreign missionary and the salaries coming from national sources will on that account be much lower. (Soltau, *Missions*, p. 22)

Again, quoting a Korean pastor, he writes, "Since that [mission] money has been practically done away with, the people in those churches have begun to realize that after all the churches are theirs and the responsibility is theirs to see that the churches are maintained properly and grow. As a result, an entirely new spirit of initiative and of forward-looking planning has come about and things are really on the move" (p. 94).

It is the realization of individual responsibility that awakens interest and stirs enthusiasm for the forward progress of the work of the Lord. Deprive the new converts of seeing visibly before them the need of their pastor, if he is to be free to do his work of shepherding and evangelizing in their community, and they will be deprived of experiencing the joy of sacrificial giving for they will not see its necessity. Rather, their new spirit of willing effort, initiative, and Christian giving, springing from gratitude and joy at their salvation, will be increasingly enfeebled due to the lack of a pressing situation calling for its utmost display. I witnessed a vivid illustration of this on one occasion in Japan. A senior seminary student was in charge of a new group that had begun as the result of summer tent evangelism. The strong Japanese tradition of ministers not emphasizing Christian giving inhibited him from doing so to a great extent. When he graduated, however, he determined he would be a living illustration to his people of their need of supporting the Lord's servant with their personal offerings. He, therefore, turned down the offer of a missionary to support him as a part-time translator and decided he would live on what the people gave him, which at that time was the equivalent of $2.80 a month, scarcely enough to provide a man for a week on a stringent diet. His testimony later was that at first it was rugged indeed. Not until his people noticed how thin and pale he was getting, and realized that his total support was what they were giving him, did they begin to open their purse strings. Then suddenly the church's monthly income began to soar, not only for the pastor but for the work of evangelism also for which he was so obviously sacrificing. The next summer that church's own offerings for summer evangelism more than equaled the rest of the presbytery's churches put together, one individual contributing a third of her income.

A church dependent upon foreign funds will also be handicapped in its evangelistic expansion work. If the people feel little incentive to give because the money is being provided anyway, then the church's evangelistic potential will be automatically curtailed. It will obviously be limited to the amount of funds that can be supplied by the mission, whereas an indigenous church's potential, dependent on the voluntary witness of Bible-class trained laymen, has no limit to the possibility of expansion save that of the number of its members. Furthermore, when all the funds are supplied from the outside, the people may well become indifferent to the administration of their church's affairs and to the work of their pastor, feeling that these responsibilities belong to the one who is paying the bills.

Thus, we see a second area in which the misuse of foreign funds create harmful effects, in the relation of the pastor to the church. The pastor who receives his salary from a missionary will be very apt to look to that missionary rather than to his people in making plans for the church. It will be very difficult for him to make decisions that he and his people feel are for the best interests of the church when the missionary differs. Increasingly, he will become dependent on the older missionary and, thus, forfeit the opportunity of developing leadership ability through the experience of leading and making decisions that ought to be his. Further, the paying of pastors or evangelists to carry on the work not only discourages laymen from volunteering their services, thus hampering evangelism, but also, not infrequently, promotes a spirit of lethargy in the evangelist who feels he is working for the mission or missionary rather than realizing he is working for the Lord and His Church. A missionary-paid native worker will almost invariably be paid on a relatively high scale, as the missionary well knows, because of his own higher standard of living, that he will open himself to criticism and resentment if he does not do so. This relative affluence, especially in the Orient, is very likely to have a subtle influence on the worker's mind, and that of the community, moving him to accept the Oriental outlook of a well-paid religious leader being a "teaching scholar" who does not mix with the people but prepares addresses to give them. This outlook makes it difficult for him to come down to the level of the people and be diligent in day-to-day evangelistic efforts such as house-to-house calling, tract distribution and street preaching.

A third area of relationships that is frequently damaged by paying national preachers is that between the missionary and the pastor. As has been noted, it encourages missionary domination with the worker being inclined to look first to please the one responsible for his salary. This in turn is apt to promote suppressed resentment on the part of the people and pastor towards the missionary upon whom they have to depend to such an extent. Nor is this practice good for the missionary himself, for he too will be tempted to lean on his paid assistant and to do less evangelistic work and language study than he should. Paying more than one assistant will lead him even farther afield, calling for more and more of his time as an administrator resulting in still less evangelistic effort on his part. The employing of an assistant by a new missionary, to help him in his language study and to get oriented to the new situations around him, for his first two or three years, is of course justifiable, but the hiring of ordained pastors or of converts to take charge of the work and do the work of evangelism is quite different.

A final area of relationships where the witness of national workers being paid by foreign funds is harmful is that involving the native populace. A foreign-paid worker promotes the idea in the community that Christianity is a foreign religion, impossible of a natural growth or acceptance in their land. In lands where nationalistic feeling runs high, such a worker is likely to bring the contempt of the community upon him for pursuing a religion that he has to be paid by foreign funds to follow. A striking conclusion to this matter can be brought in the observation of an experienced Korea missionary, "I am convinced that the amount of anti-foreign feeling can nearly always be expected in exact proportion to the amount of foreign funds used. The more foreign funds used in the work, the more anti-foreign sentiment you are likely to have" (Hodges, p. 7).

Building Funds

Many of the reasons already given against the advisability of the use of foreign funds for paying evangelistic assistants also apply against such funds being used to build church buildings for Christian groups. Such expenditure deprives the Christians of seeing the need and experiencing the joy of sacrificial giving, of discovering their potential for united accomplishment, of the satisfaction of personal ownership and of feeling the necessity for real Christian stewardship for the church's forward progress. A small chapel built by their own efforts means far more to a small group than a fine one built by foreign funds, especially if they have had to wait for some years, meeting in homes or rented halls while they gave sacrificially to the building fund. A missionary on this continent has testified, "Some of our congregations in Central America have struggled for ten years to build their chapels. They have begun in a private home, moved into a thatch-roofed hut of their own, and finally after years of sacrifice and labor, have completed their frame or adobe building. Their little chapel means infinitely more to them than if it had been provided by the mission" (Hodges, p. 69). Such self-built chapels will furnish a lasting demonstration to themselves and the community of what the church can do through united, sacrificial effort and are a constant challenge to go on to further accomplishments.

On the other hand, the mission-built chapel will be a lasting witness of a bad example to other groups who will also expect help and thus have their initiative and spirit of giving damaged. If the missionary who pursues this practice is working with an already established denomination, older, self-supporting pastors who have not yet been able to erect a building may resent it as unfair if only new groups formed by a missionary are given this aid and they are ignored. The redeemed man is still subject to such feelings, with the disharmony which ensues, for "we have this treasure in earthen vessels" (2 Cor. 4:7). The mission-built chapel is also exposed to the community's conclusion that Christianity is a foreign religion requiring large sums of foreign money to survive, a hot-house plant that will wither when the artificial heat is turned off. Further, such expenditures, especially since under the western eyes of missionary supervision the building will almost certainly be much more elaborate than necessary for a young church, will require large outlays of money, which could be better spent in sending missionaries to new fields.

Loaning a large sum to a small church group for a fine building, to be repaid on the installment plan over a considerable period of years, is subject to many of the same liabilities and some others. The more it is done, the larger are the sums of money tied up that could be better used in sending out new missionaries to new fields. The young church is burdened with a debt, unnecessarily large because of the western style and proportions, which may take them a generation to repay. The young congregation is thus tied to the foreign mission in an unhealthy way with the possibility of considerable tension developing if they later find it difficult to make the payments or decide they should move to another location. If the mission cancels the payments in such circumstances then the path to a gift-church is renewed and the temptation set for other groups likewise to ask for cancellation of payments. If difficulties arise between the missionary or the foreign-paid pastor and the people, they will be quicker to go elsewhere feeling little responsibility for the building for which they have made such little contribution. Thus it can be said that the whole morale of those seeking to follow the methods of the indigenous system can be jeopardized by such church building policy.

Not infrequently a missionary finds that what he has begun as a Bible class in his home has developed into a regular church worship service. Here, too, since he is providing all the facilities, he will find that he is jeopardizing the indigenous growth of the church, but that he has begun something it is difficult to escape from. I had such an experience, and, for a number of years, the large living-dining room was used by the growing church and the Japanese pastor to whom it was turned over. None of the members had a room large enough to hold the meetings and I was very reluctant to raise an embarrassing situation by insisting that the church move to its own quarters. Finally, I did tell them that it would be much to their advantage to find their own place and that the move would doubtless bring new people into the meetings, and I suggested to them three months to accomplish it. A rented hall was found, the move was made and efforts to expand the building fund undertaken. A couple of years later, they were able to use their building fund to make a much more advantageous move and were completely on their own.

The fields of building hospitals or higher educational institutions can be extremely expensive ones for a mission to enter. If they are to be entered, it would seem wise to do so only where there are no adequate facilities available, and then on a moderate scale. The realization must ever be kept in the foreground that the groundwork of an indigenous church is being laid. What is built must be on a scale that the church can be expected to maintain at some future time, perhaps not so far distant if circumstances should arise necessitating the withdrawal of all missionaries.

The missionary's attitude towards the indigenous system, however, must not be that of always saying "no" to opportunities to invest foreign funds in the Lord's work on the field. Indigenous principles do not call for only a negative response to all appeals for progress and advance in which funds are required. How then can mission funds be properly used?

Helping the cause of training theological students for the ministry is certainly one proper use of mission funds. The higher education of ministers is a paramount necessity, especially in this day of the wide advance of sophisticated unbelief and attacks on conservative Christianity. A theological seminary, one of the early requisites of a developing indigenous church, is usually one of the last things an indigenous church can be expected fully to finance because of the necessity of first achieving self-support of the local churches and their multiplication through evangelism. Thus foreign funds can properly be used here. Even in Korea, usually recognized to be the finest example of indigenous church growth, foreign funds greatly aided the start and maintenance of the theological seminary.

Yet here again the expenditures must be undertaken carefully, the institution being run not on a western scale but with a view to the church taking it over later on a standard of upkeep they can afford. The churches must be educated to appreciate their relation to the seminary as the source of their future pastors, needing their financial contributions, a basic necessity for the development of the work, responsibility for which they must be willing to assume as early as possible.

Translation and Publication Funds

The field of literature is another one in which foreign financial aid can wisely be used. The translation and publication of good literature for the education of the people and ministers is of the greatest importance. A cooperative work with native Christian scholars, the mission offering men with know-how and funds to do the work, is a laudable enterprise. Where an inadequate translation of the Bible exists, due to modern influences or some other, and the Bible Society is unwilling to undertake a revision, foreign funds may have to be raised and put at the disposal of a committee of native scholars and missionaries to see that a good translation of God's Word is available. The stocking and maintaining of lending libraries of good books as well as subsidizing the price of more expensive ones that are to be sold, so that they can be widely used, contribute to the wise use of funds. Such books as Bible commentaries, dictionaries, concordances, and lexicons are usually quite expensive for the convert on the mission field unless a price, sometimes lower than cost, is set on them. Yet here again, as in Bible distribution work, the books will be much more appreciated, and therefore receive more consideration, if a price is paid for them rather than being given away. The preparation, renting, and sale of audio-visual materials, as well as the making of tapes for radio broadcasting and the financing of the station broadcasts, also is a proper use of foreign contributions.

When in primitive areas dispensaries are operated or simple hospitals built, the need of turning these over to the church eventually must be kept in mind. Although, of course, adequate standards of cleanliness and hygiene must be maintained, yet the structure and its common facilities need not be patterned on western standards but rather made to fit in with the living customs of the people. Preparation for turning the operation over to a native Christian administration must be begun years in advance, including training in democratic governmental methods, sense of responsibility for property, and eventual full administration. Welfare work where disease or disaster on a large scale is involved, with which the national church cannot possibly cope, likewise is an area where foreign Christian funds may well be used, care being taken that a clear witness for Christ accompanies it.

In addition to the above, however, there are many instances that will arise where new, good projects need encouragement and judicious contributions may be given, but always on a small scale. A contribution to the building fund or a special evangelistic effort, of course, may be made by the missionary, but a good rule of thumb is never to let such exceed ten percent of the total cost of the enterprise.

The Bible Front and Center

The basic motive for self-support of a new church, as has already been said, must be that the Word of God may be preached to its own people and to their neighbors, for the glory of God and the salvation of the lost, as far out as they can reach, if they are to go on growing after reaching that goal, and be a rising sun in a dark land. The real key to achieving this end then lies in the inner life of the church members, and the source of that life lies in a personal relationship to Christ of saving faith and obedience to His will as it is revealed in the infallible Scriptures. Thus knowledge of the Bible is basic to the development of a self-supporting church that is really a church of Jesus Christ.

From the very beginning, then, intensive Bible training is essential if a self-supporting, indigenous church is to be produced. All too often when speaking of the "Nevius Plan" the basic factor that such Bible training is the very foundation of it is overlooked. Without question the remarkable success attained in Korea in developing an indigenous church was due to the fullest realization of this central place of Bible knowledge and the extremely efficient system developed for imparting Bible instruction. Sunday school attendance involved the whole church with the Bible as the text in every class. In addition, adult members were trained as Sunday school teachers, and to be more efficient witnesses for Christ, in special Bible training courses held in some centrally located church and lasting all day for from five to twelve days. Further, the larger mission stations erected buildings and conducted Bible institutes in them during the winter months, when the country people were relatively inactive, which lasted from one to two-and-a-half months. The students paid their own expenses and were given courses covering the whole Bible as well as instruction in church activities, Sunday school teaching, Christian stewardship, the work of elders, church discipline, and methods of evangelism and of caring for church finances. Thus an army of volunteer lay workers, who continued in their own vocation and were the backbone of the church, was trained, the source of the remarkable growth of the indigenous church in Korea.

As to methods of financing the self-support of a new church, the tithe is definitely the best plan since ten families can support a pastor on the scale of their average income. If the tithe is pledged to the church it helps the church prepare an annual budget. Paul, in instructing the young church of Corinth, emphasized proportionate giving. "Upon the first day of the week let every one of you lay by him in store, as God hath prospered him, that there be no gathering when I come" (1 Cor. 16:2). The tenth is an example given in the Bible for giving to the Lord's work. When church members have adopted this method of giving, churches have made tremendous strides toward full support. An illustration is given of a church in Brazil. "The analysis of church income showed that 26 tithing members of a total membership of 640 were contributing three-fourths of the whole budget. When this was made clear to the congregation, 54 other persons began the practice of tithing and the church was lifted to a self-supporting position" (Davis, *How the Church Grows in Brazil,* p. 198).

In rural communities, where money is scarce, giving part of the produce of the farm to the pastor's support may be necessary. Sometimes a tithe of the produce is given while at others a portion of the farm's land is allocated and all produced on it is given to the church. In modern communities today, when a young native seminary graduate is seeking to begin a new church, it may be necessary for him to take some kind of part-time employment as Paul did in making tents in Corinth. Sometimes this can be profitably linked to the making of new contacts for the gospel as when the pastor tutors high school students preparing for important exams or teaches English or music. But from the very beginning of the new church, the principles of self-support must be taught and the fact made plain that the part-time employment of the pastor is a temporary measure. In Korea, a satisfactory system was worked out where single churches, too small to provide the entire salary of a pastor, formed circuits with other small churches with the elders leading the services and presenting the Word in the intervals between pastoral visits.

Where there are seminary students available who could preach for and help develop small churches, which might be unable to pay a full salary, this arrangement is very appropriate and mutually helpful. When I had been in a rural community in Japan for ten months, I was asked to go 300 miles north to Tokyo to help organize a theological seminary. A small church had been started with five baptized converts, a small group of enquirers, and a Sunday school of about 50, meeting in the rented home where the missionary family lived. When I announced to the group that I would have to move to Tokyo, the landlady, an elderly widow and one of the most earnest Christians, said, "But now the work will fall apart!" I replied that the Lord would be still with them and that I would try to come for one Sunday a month, and get another missionary to attend one Sunday a month. For the other two Sundays they would be left to their own resources around the Word. The Sunday school was the most adversely affected, dropping to about a dozen, but almost at once real leadership ability began to develop in a young farmer who was attending night high school, and later he was ordained as an elder. The next year, a seminary student began to go in place of the missionaries and the church group began to assume the expense. By the time this young man graduated, the church paid him for coming three times a month, and later he was called to be their pastor. Today, this group is fully self-supporting, has an ordained pastor, and contributes to the work of the presbytery and the seminary. A fitting remark with which to close is simply this affirmation: God's work, done by God's men in God's way, will have God's support.

Questions for Study and Discussion

1. What four aspects of the work of the Church should be supported by the church itself to make it truly a self-supported church? In what order is this support usually undertaken by the church itself?

2. What two tests did John Nevius suggest to evaluate missionary methods?

3. What are some advantages of self-support from inception for a church? Is this possible?

4. What areas of church and missionary work are apt to be hindered when a church receives foreign aid?

5. Should a missionary start a church in his own home? Give reasons for your answer.

6. How can mission funds be properly used on the foreign field?

7. What is most basic to building an indigenous self-supporting church? Why?

Bibliography

Aalders, G. Charles. *Calvinism in Times of Crisis*. Grand Rapids: Baker, 1947.

Adeney, David H. *The Unchanging Commission*. Chicago: InterVarsity Press, 1955.

Allen, R. *Essential Missionary Principles*. New York: Revell, 1913.

---. *Missionary Methods: St. Paul's or Ours*. London: Scott, 1927.

---. *The Spontaneous Expansion of the Church*. London: Scott, 1949.

Anderson, Gerald H., ed. *The Theology of the Christian Mission*. New York: McGraw-Hill, 1961.

Azariah, V. S. "Self-Support: False and True," *International Review of Missions*, Vol. 27, 1938.

Bates, M. Searle. *Religious Liberty, Church and State*. New York: Missionary Research Library, 1959.

Bavinck, J. H. *The Impact of Christianity in the Non-Christian World*. Grand Rapids: Eerdmans, 1948.

---. *An Introduction to the Science of Missions*. Grand Rapids: Baker, 1960.

Beyerhaus, Peter and Henry Lefever. *The Responsible Church and the Foreign Mission*. Grand Rapids: Eerdmans, 1965.

Boer, Harry R. *That My House May Be Filled*. Grand Rapids: Eerdmans, 1957.

---. *Pentecost and Missions*. Grand Rapids: Eerdmans, 1961

Bunce, W. K. *Religions in Japan, Buddhism, Shinto, Christianity*. Tokyo: C. E. Tuttle Co., 1955.

Clark, C. A. *The Nevius Plan for Mission Work*. Korea: Christian Literature Crusade.

Clark, S. J. W. *The Indigenous Church.* World Dominion Press, 1928.

Cook, Harold R. *An Introduction to the Study of Christian Missions.* Chicago: Moody Press, 1954.

---. *The Theology of Evangelism: The Gospel in the World of Today.* London: Corey Kingsgate, 1951.

Davis, J. Merle. *The Economic Basis of the Church*, Madras Series, Vol. V, International Missionary Council, 1939.

---. *The Economic and Social Environment of the Younger Churches.* Edinburgh Press, 1939.

---. *New Buildings on Old Foundations.* International Missionary Council, 1947.

---. *The Cuban Church in a Sugar Economy.* International Missionary Council, 1942.

---. *The Economic Basis of the Evangelical Church in Mexico.* International Missionary Council, 1940.

---. *How the Church Grows in Brazil.* International Missionary Council, 1943.

Glasser, Arthur F. *Missions in Crisis.* London: InterVarsity, 1961.

Greene, E. B. *Church and State.* National Foundation Press, 1947.

Grubb, Kenneth G. *The Church and the State.* England: Oxford University Press, 1938.

Haskin, Dorothy G. "They Go To Bed Less Hungry," *United Evangelical Action,* April 1961.

Hodges, Melvin L. *On the Mission Field: The Indigenous Church.* Chicago: Moody Press, 1953.

Huizinga, A.V. C. P. *The Calvinist View of the State.* Holland: V/H Brofse & Peereboom, 1933.

Judd, Walter. "Congressman Judd Talks to Young People About Politics," *United Evangelical Action,* April 1961.

Kraemer, H. *The Christian Message in a Non-Christian World.* New York: Harper, 1938.

---. *The Communication of the Christian Faith.* Philadelphia: Westminster

Press, 1956.

Kuyper, Abraham. *Calvinism: Six Stone Foundation Lectures*. Grand Rapids: Eerdmans, 1943

Lamott, W. *Revolution in Missions*. New York: MacMillan, 1954.

Lindsell, Harold. *A Christian Philosophy of Missions*. Wheaton: VanKampen, 1949.

---. *Missionary Principles and Practice*. Westwood, N.J.: Revell, 1955.

Manikan, R. B. "A New Era in the World Mission of the Church," *Union Seminary Quarterly Review*, Nov. 1937, Vol. XIII, No. 1.

Matsushita, Dr. *The Bible Times*, Vol. 9, No. 3, 1959.

Meeter, H. Henry. *Calvinism*. Grand Rapids: Zondervan, 1939.

Moody Symposium. *Facing Facts in Modern Missions*. Chicago: Moody Press, 1963.

Neill, Stephen. *The Unfinished Task*. London: Lutterworth, 1957.

---. *A History of Christian Missions*. Grand Rapids: Eerdmans, 1965.

Nevius, John L. *Planting and Development of Missionary Churches*. Grand Rapids: Baker, 1899.

"New Model Missionary," *The Cape Breton Post, Weekend Magazine*, Vol. 11, No. 19, 1961.

Oishi, Dr. Y. *Religion and State in Japan*. Tokyo, 1959.

Ono, Dr. Sokyo. *The Kami Way: An Introduction to Shrine Shinto*. Tokyo, 1959.

Soltau, Theodore Stanley. *Missions at the Crossroads: The Indigenous Church*. Grand Rapids: Baker, 1955.

---. *Facing the Field*. Grand Rapids: Baker, 1959.

Tamura, Y. *Living Buddhism in Japan*. Tokyo: International Institute for Study of Religions, 1959.

Thomsen, Harry. "Sokka Gakai." *Japanese Religions*, Vol. 1, No. 2. Tokyo: The Christian Center for the Study of Japanese Religions, 1959.

Uchimura, K. *How I Became a Christian*. Tokyo, 1895.

Vos, J. G. *Christian Missions and the Civil Magistrate in the Far East.* Tokyo: Japan Bible Christian Council (reprint from *Westminster Theological Journal.*)

Yanagita, Tomonobu. *Short History of Christianity in Japan.* Tokyo: Bible Library Publishers, 1957.

---. "The Christian as a Witness for Freedom in Japan," *The Bible Times,* Vol. 9, No. 2. Tokyo, 1959.

Yoshiro, Tamura. *Living Buddhism in Japan: A report of interviews with ten Japanese Buddhist leaders.* Tokyo, 1972.

Young, John M.L. *The Two Empires in Japan.* Tokyo, Nuttley, N.J.: The Presbyterian & Reformed Publishing Co., 1959.

Zwemer, Samuel M. *Thinking Missions with Christ.* Grand Rapids: Zondervan, 1935.

Presence of books in this bibliography does not mean endorsement.

The body text for *Missions: The Biblical Motive
and Aim* is set in 10.5 Hoefler Text. Chapter titles are
set in Helvetica Neue.

Missions: The Biblical Motive and Aim was typeset
and designed on an Apple Macintosh operating system using Adobe InDesign and Adobe Photoshop.

The cover art—*He Himself is Our Peace*—is by
Nicora N. Gangi. It is based on Ephesians 2:14-17.
Verse 17 says, "He came and preached peace to you
who were far away and peace to those who were
near." Those who are on missions are bringing His
peace to people everywhere, and building bridges to
destroy "the barrier, the dividing wall of hostility."

Other Titles from
Crown and Covenant Publications

Genesis by J. G. Vos

The 166 lessons originally appeared in his theological journal *Blue Banner Faith and Life*. With review questions at the end of each lesson, this book is useful for personal or group study. Vos, known for his teachable style, writes in a way that is accessible for the layperson.

Paper, 544 pp. BS210 $20; Hard/dustcover, 544 pp. BS211 $32

Faith of Our Fathers by Wayne Spear

Faith of Our Fathers helps today's reader understand the *Westminster Confession of Faith* written over 350 years ago. Spear gives just enough historical background and paragraph-by-paragraph commentary to help the average layperson glean all the treasures the *Confession* supplies.

Paper, 176 pp. DS188 $8

Sing the Lord's Song by John Keddie

Easy-to-read book about singing the psalms of the Bible in worship. This defense of exclusive psalmody is thoughtful, respectful, and simple. A must-read for anyone interested in the topic of worship song.

Paper, 74 pp. DS213 $6

Understanding Biblical Doctrine

Because of its simple and inductive approach, *Understanding Biblical Doctrine* has been a popular workbook in theology for more than 25 years with new believers, communicant students, and mature Christians. Each lesson takes you to the Scriptures to find what God says about Himself, creation, man, sin, the plan of salvation, the Christian life, and more.

Paper, 80 pp. DS220 $10

www.crownandcovenant.com